D0862538

SOUTHBOUND ON THE
APPALACHIAN TRAIL

SOUTHBOUND ON THE APPALACHIAN TRAIL

By Ken Sarzynski

PARDON MY PUBLISHING

ARLINGTON

Southbound on the Appalachian Trail
Written by Ken Sarzynski

Copyright © 2010 by Ken Sarzynski

Cover design, photographs, and images by Ken Sarzynski

All cover and interior images copyright © 2010 by Ken Sarzynski

All rights reserved. No part of this book may be used or reproduced in any manner whatsoever, without written permission from the publisher, except in the case of reprints in the context of reviews.

Published By: Pardon My Publishing ™
                  www.PardonMyPublishing.com

ISBN-13: 978-0615424101
ISBN-10: 0615424104

Cover Photo: Clouds roll down from Mount Washington and settle around the rustic Lake of the Clouds Hut. A solitary hiker contemplates the view while waiting for dinner time.

This book is dedicated to the memory of my grandpa, John Sarzynski, who showed me that, given enough time and patience, anything is possible. The family still can't figure out how you rearranged all that furniture by yourself.

Special thanks to Cate Christiaanse and Andrea Sarzynski for helping me produce the book you are reading now.

Contents

Top: Starting June 15, 2007, atop Mount Katahdin in Maine. A gorgeously beautiful, clear, sunny day without a cloud in the sky. My toes wanted to say "Hello" in true Spock fashion.

Right: Posing for a photo on October 30, 2007, outside the visitors center in Amicalola State Park in Georgia. The symbol on the stone, of an A on top of a T, is synonymous with "Appalachian Trail". This was my official "I'm finished!" postcard for friends and family.

"SOBOMEGA" is shorthand for "Southbound, Maine to Georgia."

"Kenneth"
June 15 to
October 30, 2007
SOBOMEGA

1. Preface

On June 14, 2007, I hopped in the passenger seat of my friend Adam's car and together we left our upstate New York homes - the trunk contained two 40 pound backpacks. Our destination was seven hours away in Monson, Maine where we would leave his vehicle and hop in his father's truck to continue on to a hotel in Millinocket. That night we ate dinner at the exquisitely situated Rock River Restaurant some distance down a non-descript dirt road. I ordered lobster-stuffed grilled haddock that was delicious. However, it was ever more succulent when I realized that this would be my last real meal for well over a week and, for all I knew, maybe the next four and a half months.

We dined in splendor, chatted like old friends, and speculated about the journey ahead. After dinner, Adam and I returned to our hotel room where we made sure we had all our gear, food, and water ready for the morning. THIS was the moment I started my hike from Maine to Georgia.

The next morning Adam's father chauffeured us to Baxter State Park where we said goodbye to him and their family dog, and checked in with the kind ranger at Katahdin Stream Campground. At 7am on June 15, I officially entered the record books as a southbound Appalachian Trail (AT) "thru-hiker" and Adam signed his intention to tackle Maine's 100 Mile Wilderness. Perhaps THIS is a more fitting start to my hike from Maine to Georgia?

From the ranger station we were told to expect 10 days of hiking before we again hit civilization in Monson, Maine. All told, from Monson I was figuring on another 120 days before I reached Springer Mountain in Georgia and could call my journey complete. I could only guess at my average pace and could only hope there would be no medical emergencies.

When I think about these early days, I can see just how naive I was. Not in a bad way, thankfully, but in a way that I was comfortable with. I had read five books about the trail, countless websites and online forums. I was no stranger to the Eastern US, its mountains or the outdoors, and I certainly was no novice when it came to camping. However, the most I had ever backpacked was six days, and the most I had ever toured by bicycle was eight days. I simply didn't know what to expect, whether I was packing the right items, or if I'd ultimately enjoy this adventure.

I wanted my hike to be educational. I wanted to put aside any fear of nature or solitude that comes from growing up in civilization. I wanted to push myself to my limits. Heck, I wanted to FIND my limits! It was impossible to fathom the breadth and depth of this undertaking, no matter how many times I ran the numbers - I would burn 4,000-6,000 calories a day while taking five million steps to cover 2,200 miles through 14 United States.

Was I really ready for this?

Like most southbound hikers, or Southbounders, on the Appalachian Trail, Adam and I spent the first day hiking to the top of Mount Katahdin with lightly outfitted day packs borrowed from the ranger station. We were lucky to reach the summit on one of those rare days when visibility was almost perfect – allowing us to see clear to the horizon. While the mountain was accommodating us with a view, the sun was leaving us with temporary tattoos to commemorate the day. We would spend some time on the summit, near the official starting point of the AT, before returning back to camp for the night. In the morning we would pack up and begin walking south towards, and through, the aptly named 100 Mile Wilderness.

On June 16, 2007, I began hiking away from the summit of Mount Katahdin and by the end of October I would be celebrating in Georgia with a 1 liter bottle of Dr. Pepper.

While hiking the AT and thinking about this book, two things came to mind. First, people asked me a lot of questions, and I felt that if they were asking them they must be important. Even folks who had read books on the AT and followed all the online forums found they had questions that nobody ever answered. I wanted to write a book that spoke to the inquiring mind and would hopefully fill what I perceive as a void among Appalachian Trail literature.

The other realization was that all the bookshelves were significantly lacking in Southbounder influence. The challenge, therefore, was to write a book that could accurately portray this unique experience, while simultaneously providing insights about the Northbounder journey and what the differences and commonalities might be. Without thinking things through, for example, a Southbounder (also known as a "Sobo") might easily complete the trail thinking every Northbounder (or "Nobo") is a liar. Why did they tell me that I would DEFINITELY see LOTS of bears in New Jersey when I didn't even see bear droppings? Where were the oh-so-common all-you-can-eat picnics and trail-side coolers full of refreshments? Where did all those wonderful, crisp, clear flowing springs I'd heard about disappear to?

This book is a reflection of my experiences and opinions. When possible, I try to share different points of view, not just my own. I am not declaring myself an expert, nor am I saying that there is only one way to do something. The point of this book is show you that, while I definitely had my own approach to hiking, there are many other methods that work - and don't work. It is up to you to find your own groove.

In my opinion, by hiking the Appalachian Trail, one is more appropriately labeled a teacher than a hiker.

2. The Trail

What is the Appalachian Trail?

The Appalachian Trail, or AT, or the Trail, is a protected 2,100-2,200 mile corridor along various sections of the Appalachian Mountains through Maine, New Hampshire, Vermont, Massachusetts, Connecticut, New York, New Jersey, Pennsylvania, Maryland, West Virginia, North Carolina, Tennessee, and Georgia. It runs from the top of Mount Katahdin (pronounced kuh-TAH-din) in Maine to the summit of Springer Mountain in Georgia.

The Appalachian Trail's primary custodian is the Appalachian Trail Conservancy (ATC). The ATC is a volunteer organization formed in 1925 (then called the Appalachian Trail Conference) that works closely with federal agencies and local groups to maintain the AT and educate the community. Their headquarters is in Harpers Ferry, just a short distance from the Trail.

You will not be relying purely on hotels, motels, restaurants or spas to get through the AT. It is often considered an introduction to long-distance backpacking because of its proximity to civilization, the relative lack of logistics required, and the number of people you are likely to encounter on any given day.

To claim you are a "thru-hiker" is to label yourself as someone intending to hike the entire length of the AT. To call yourself a Northbounder or Southbounder is to indicate the overall direction you are traveling.

Around 90% of Appalachian Trail thru-hikers start off in Georgia and hike north to Maine, so it's natural that most of the books, videos and online resources are told from that perspective. For someone traveling the opposite direction, as I was, it therefore came as no surprise to learn that my experiences were drastically different from what I had read. Even the souvenirs available along the Trail reflect this with tee-shirts pointing out the "Georgia TO Maine" direction of the Trail or mugs reminding the drinker that the Trail goes from south to north. On the one hand this helped my wallet (since I wasn't going to support such inaccurate merchandise), on the other hand it reinforced the idea that starting in Maine was somehow abnormal. But then I would leave the shop with a smile on my face as I remembered that it's fun to be different.

The AT is forever changing as land is constantly being acquired and trail is always being relocated. The year that I hiked the AT, the official length was 2,187 miles. After all the detours, off-trail camping, stumbling, and potty breaks, I simply call it 2,200. You can label it a trail, but in reality there's a fair bit of walking on roads and bridges. Sometimes it's located, unseen, on a distant ridge, tucked away where nobody would ever notice; or maybe you'll find yourself walking past a dozen fenced yards with barking dogs and stereos blasting. Why are there AT symbols and blazes (painted marks) going down Main Street? Well, my dear, that there is the Appalachian Trail. But don't get me wrong; you are hiking, you will get dirty, you will be camping, and you will be roughing it.

It is - and this is VERY important to note - a well populated footpath. It passes through and near towns, national and state parks, major highways, private camps, and crosses many rivers and streams. Some would consider it a rugged outdoor experience, but, due to its proximity to so many populated areas, it is far from remote. In 2007, there were approximately 1,200 hikers starting in Georgia with 312 finishing in Maine. Conversely, there were around 200 Southbounders starting in Maine and somewhere around 40 that reached Georgia. These approximations are based on the AT Conservancy website and information from the headquarters in Harpers Ferry, which rely on hikers signing a ledger at the start and end of the Trail.

And, if you don't think you saw that many people as you hiked throughout the day, wait till you get to camp that night. Even though hikers generally start over a one to three month window of time, it's not uncommon for a Northbounder to find a shelter with 70 people packed in and around it, or 50 people in and around a shelter as you head south. Mostly the numbers are higher the closer you are to the start of the Trail.

There's a lot of fascinating history to the Trail that few people ask about - not because they have no interest, but probably because they don't think there IS a history. I wish I could go in to the details, but I'm more than happy to leave the history lesson to other books. In general, somebody asking me "What is the AT?" didn't want me to tell them who created it or how it came to be, it was really just an innocent way of saying "No, seriously, I don't understand what you're doing. I REALLY have no clue what you're talking about. Are you homeless???"

Hey, did you read that book?

From people that knew of the AT, the number one question I heard was "Did you read that book?" Some people could recall the title and/or author and some had to be prompted by me for that information, but either way it was usually the conversation starter. It was as if talking about the book with an Appalachian Trail thru-hiker allowed them to share in the experience and heighten their enjoyment.

I'd wager that most people alive today only know about the AT because of Bill Bryson's controversial (sigh) 1998 book, *A Walk in the Woods*, based on his incomplete attempt to hike the Trail. I heard "Wow, the Appalachian Trail? Hey, did you read that book by Bill Bryson?" so many times that I would make a game out of guessing how long it would take someone to bring it up in the conversation.

Even if it does make me the target of ridicule among thru-hikers, I'll gladly go on record to say that I enjoyed his book immensely. Believe it or not, this is a very touchy subject among thru-hikers.

In the book, Bill recounts his attempt to hike the Trail and does so in both a humorous and informative way. He goes into rich details about the local histories and various intriguing destinations. It's a story of physical, mental and social struggle and very accurately reflects what a person is likely to experience on the AT.

Here's where it gets ugly - and hopefully this doesn't ruin the book for you - Bryson does not finish all 2,000+ miles of the AT and apparently this royally irks many people! They feel cheated, like Bryson was lying to them just so he could profit from the Trail. I met a fellow that claimed Bill was fabricating stories just to make "the South" look bad, and a few hikers claimed that some of his stories couldn't have been true, simply because in all their worldly travels nothing like that ever happened to them. These statements were always made in an agitated fashion, which did nothing to boost the credibility of the speaker.

Just say the name "Bryson" around camp and all you'll hear for the next hour is a heated argument about his book.

And it wasn't even false advertising! The title isn't "I Hiked the Entire AT" or "What 2,100 Miles Feels Like" for Heaven's sake. Most importantly, there's a 70-90% drop-out rate for AT hikers, many don't even make it past 100 miles, and here's a man that manages 500 miles and you're calling him a cheat?

Furthermore, the overwhelming feeling on the Trail is, no matter how far you make it, you've still accomplished a great deal, and the concept of "failure" doesn't even exist. Success on the AT is largely defined as "getting as far as fate decides," since the biggest step one can take, of the 5 million from Maine to Georgia, is the step away from home. So why burn a book that is representative of 70-90% of thru-hikers?

The simple fact is, whether you liked the book or not, you cannot deny how effective it was in getting people out of their homes and into the woods. It's how I, and my family for that matter, first really learned about the Trail. Oh sure, we knew that near our home there was a foot bridge over a highway that said "Appalachian Trail," but it was just some vague notion before Bill came along to define it for us.

Sometimes I think thru-hikers should be issued donkeys at the start of the Trail so they're less likely to get on a high-horse.

Because many people I met were curious, I will say that Bill's book is quite accurate from a thru-hiker perspective. In Georgia, it is common to find gear strewn about the side of the Trail as people discard unneeded items in an attempt to lose weight. Friendships are put to a test, and even in this day and age with easy access to information, you will find people that are unprepared for the trip and forced to learn along the way.

One aspect of the book really gets people thinking, and I was often asked if my experience in the 100 Mile Wilderness was anything like Bill's.

In the book, he jumps ahead to the end of the AT in Maine to see what it's like. In the 1990's, this section of Trail was very different than it is today. Bog crossings didn't all have the convenience of wooden walkways, and, on at least one occasion, he recounts having to carry his pack above his head as he waded across one. Because of the book, so many people came to the Wilderness and the number of rescues and emergency evacuations rose so much that the park had to introduce various measures to counteract the problem – like improving trail conditions, posting disclaimers and using rangers to look for and stop potentially unqualified hikers from entering. Today the friendly rangers in Baxter State Park may give you a quick inter-rogation, ask to see what you're carrying, and potentially send you back to town to mail gear home and/or make some purchases.

How long does it take? What's the record?

I'd always read that the average window for doing the Trail in either direction is 4.5 to 6.5 months. This is from start to finish and includes any time off.

While there are many instances of people doing it in significantly less time, the Appalachian Trail Conservancy does not support the idea of "records" and refuses to recognize the concept. In fact, Benton MacKeye, the father of the AT, believed that an award should be given to the person who hikes the Trail in the longest amount of time.

I met a Southbounder this year that did the Trail in about three and a half months, and I passed Northbounders on target for three months. Anywhere from 40 days to 90 days isn't unusual. Most people would be traveling so light that car support would be needed the entire length of the Trail, and camping would be replaced with sleeping in a vehicle or being driven to town.

Northbounders can start at any time but most wait until March for the brunt of winter to pass. You can't wait too long because winter can hit New England in October and after October 15 the state park terminus in Maine is shut down for safety reasons.

Heading south, you can't start until the park in Maine opens, usually around June 1, and since there's no such limitation down in Georgia you can take your sweet time getting there. Winter in the Smoky Mountains can be severe and dangerous, so many Southbounders try to finish before winter sets up in the south. Simultaneously, a fair number will choose a deadline of Thanksgiving in order to be home with family.

If you decide to start early or end late in the north, it's not just Baxter State Park closing or even the snow that you have to think about. Beware of "mud season" in late fall or early spring when the concern for erosion will cause many trails to close.

Me! At the official start of the AT in Maine.

Adam joined me so that he could experience the 100 Mile Wilderness first hand.

3. A Walk in Maine

Looking back on Mount Katahdin on the way to the 100 Mile Wilderness.

Length:	281 miles	452 km
Max Elevation:	5,267 feet	1,605 m
Min Elevation:	490 feet	149 m
My First Day:	June 15	
My Last Day:	July 4	

What's it like?

The Maine portion of the AT has a well deserved reputation for being rough, wild and gorgeous.

The black flies and mosquitoes can strip the paint from a pickup truck in less than an hour. OK, that's unfair for me to say, but judging by how many people asked about the biting insects in Maine, it was clear that their heads were filled with images of swarms of bugs consuming the landscape and destroying everything in their path. Maybe it was a "bad" year, maybe I'm just used to mosquitoes and biting flies, or maybe I just got lucky, but the truth is I really only had one encounter with black flies and for the most part torrents of rain kept the mosquitoes away. In comparison, I found Massachusetts to be far worse, but I certainly did meet people utterly demoralized by the mosquitoes in Maine. I got by with long sleeves, pants, and a hat while saving DEET (as close to 100% as possible!) bug spray for desperate times.

I love this state on a variety of levels and hiking is a big one. The forest is still expansive, remote, dense, and majestic. Nowhere else on the Trail did I hear the unique, surreal call of aquatic birds called loons, and the only moose I saw were in Maine (even though they can range all the way to New York). The moose droppings were everywhere and in such abundance that they pretty much made up the entire surface of the trail for dozens of yards at a time. This is not hyperbole; it's like walking through an animal pen at the zoo where the workers have been on strike for weeks. You get the impression that these towering relatives of cows have set aside these stretches just as humans would build public restrooms. At times, while walking in the early morning hours, stepping around piles of poop and collecting strands of spider silk with my face, I would suddenly encounter a stretch of trail where the webs abruptly stopped for 100 feet and just as suddenly started back up - I'm confident that a moose had walked these sections before me.

In Maine, I would rise early with the sun at 5am and within 30 minutes I would be hiking. Because I was most often the first person to leave the campground, I was also the person everyone thanked for clearing the cobwebs that formed overnight. Every day I looked forward to my first encounter with a hiker heading north, because it meant that at least for a while I wouldn't have to deal with cobwebs, and since that person would feel the same way the mutual greeting was often "Good morning. Yay, no more cobwebs!" In reality this inconvenience is not isolated to Maine; you will find it all throughout the Trail.

I found Maine to be unique, in that on at least three separate occasions I could see with such clarity over such a distance that I could make out every hill, valley, river or town that I would be hitting in the next week. The mountaintop views from other states simply didn't have the same high definition. Some came close, but what really makes Maine different is

Adam's pack and mine taking a break shortly after entering the 100 Mile Wilderness.

that each major mountain range was separated by relatively flat and visible regions. In the Smoky Mountains, for example, I could see quite a ways, but every direction seemed to be the same jumble of forested mountains.

Every other state has constructed bridges to allow for easy river crossings or placed the Trail where it could share a bridge with traffic, but in Maine that's not the case. The 100 Mile Wilderness has several significant rivers that you must ford, and I learned from fellow hikers that, if the weather was uncooperative, they could be waist deep. In my case these crossings were never deeper than my knees. The Kennebec River, half way to New Hampshire, is notoriously wicked due to unpredictable dam releases and has been known to kill hikers attempting to ford it. As a result, there is a free ferry service consisting of a canoe with one "driver" and room for two hikers that operates daily during the hiking season.

And on the topic of water bodies, Maine was brimming over with bogs, especially in the 100 Mile Wilderness. In order to safely cross them (for you and for the bogs) wood planks are suspended (sometimes precariously) over them. Often times the boards would be partly submerged, causing you to slip and nearly topple in to the water. Or they behaved like a teeter-totter and suddenly shifted their angle and sent you slipping – fortunately you learn to spot these by looking for the planks that are above water and yet somehow seem to be wet. You have to keep telling yourself that thousands of hikers this year have already crossed over and it hasn't broken for them, so it's probably sturdy enough for you. Personally, bogs frighten me because I don't know the extent of the bottoms' softness, and if I'll get stuck. Fortunately, I never "went in."

Several times, I was able to camp directly on the shore of an iso-
lated pond or lake and watch the sun set or rise over its waters. A few had portions that were reserved for some form of settlement (cabin, dock, lodge, camp, etc.) but these were generally hidden completely from view. For the most part, the Trail is removed enough from civiliza-

A sheltered lake soon after leaving the 100 Mile Wilderness.

tion that the ponds and lakes have avoided any development. They have calm waters with no light pollution and no engine noises of any kind.

The elevation changes in Maine aren't exactly insignificant, but they're not catastrophic either. The problem with the mountains here, as in most of New England, is that the Trail just tends to go straight up - as if to find the shortest route, often with the help of painstakingly crafted stone steps. The hiker joke is that when they made the AT in Maine, they hadn't yet figured out switchbacks. I have a feeling this joke is founded at least partially in reality.

Even hiking in late May or early June you can encounter snow and, if you don't, you can at least expect immense quantities of mud. New Englanders call the time after winter thaw "mud season," and even while the AT might still be open, you might be encouraged not to add to the erosion. To me, the biggest peril with hiking when there's snow on the ground is following the AT. Many sections go over mountains that are one big slab of rock and the Trail is marked by either small stone cairns (piles of rock) or white paint applied to the rock you're walking on – either of which can easily be covered with snow. You may need to budget for the extra time spent trying to figure out where the Trail goes down the mountain. I was hiking late enough that I never encountered snow, but if you leave before mid-June, you do run this risk.

A few highlights

Baxter State Park and its famous Mount Katahdin are highlights for thru-hikers and all forms of outdoor enthusiast. The trails are gorgeous, the views from Katahdin are spectacular and so are the views of Katahdin from meadows throughout the park. Before hiking the AT, this was the first and only place I had seen moose in the wild. There are many trails throughout the park available to day-hikers or campers but sometimes the more popular parking lots can fill up before 8am, so you might need to get there early.

The 100 Mile Wilderness, though time consuming and not for the inexperienced, is highly recommended primarily for the remoteness of it all. You can get better views for less work elsewhere, and you can see moose throughout much of New England, so what you are primarily getting in the 100 Mile Wilderness is isolation. There are no paved roads and only the occasional dirt road; there are very few hikers; there are no screaming babies or packs of weekend hikers or picnickers. The dark of night is free from light pollution and the stars speak directly to you. Then again, it also has a very active lumber industry and while you can't see them, you can quite often hear the rumbling of lumber trucks tearing down the other side of the valley.

If the 100 Mile Wilderness is too much for you, then perhaps you're looking for Gulf Hagas. Towards the southern end of the 100 Mile Wilderness, the Gulf is a beautiful gorge with waterfalls, pools and cliff-top trails. This was the only place in the 100 Mile Wilderness that I saw day-hikers since it is reasonably easily accessed via dirt roads.

After Katahdin, the first big mountain was Avery Peak next to Flagstaff Lake, so it was a very memorable time getting up and over it, but I also saw a good number of day-hikers on this range. It's easily accessed and while it's not an easy hike, the view from Avery is an absolutely fabulous 360 degree treat.

Mahoosuc Notch is just before the border to New Hampshire, outside of Grafton Notch State Park. If you look at a topographic map of the Notch, you will see that it's flanked by two sizeable mountains: Fulling Mill and Mahoosuc Mountain. The former is very steep, while the latter is "I need a knee replacement" steep. The Notch is a stunning example of what happens when a very precariously situated mountain breaks apart. The narrow slice of valley floor is literally full of small to bus size boulders, preventing you from ever seeing the ground and forcing you to scramble up, over, around and under massive rocks while pushing, pulling and dragging your backpack. Coming down Mahoosuc Mountain from my overnight campground at Old Speck Pond was sometimes tricky, always steep, but nothing I'd consider tough. Heading up the mountain is an entirely different affair, judging by the number of thru-hikers that claim Mahoosuc Notch to be the most difficult part of the AT.

4. The Experience

What in blazes are you talking about?

Hiking the AT means that you are generally following the white painted blazes mile after mile. But there are many ways to hike the AT and there are just as many slang terms for doing so. You might hear someone say "They didn't really hike the whole thing, they yellow blazed a lot of it," or "I'm a blue blazer," or "we decided to aqua blaze Connecticut."

To say you officially completed the AT, and get your certificate, you technically must walk every white blaze and not take any detours or skip sections. The hiking culture is split three ways on this subject: 1. I must hike the white blazes! 2. I'll hike whatever I want. 3. I'll hike the original AT!

For people hiking the original AT, the idea is quite simple: when a blue blazed side trail presents itself that happens to be part of the original, I'll take that instead of follow the white blazes. Many of the original sections of the AT went directly through towns, but

A street lamp in Vermont marked with a white blaze.

nowadays the path may skirt around them, and these older sections got re-blazed with blue paint. Even people in the "I'll hike whatever I want" category may take these trails as a short cut or more convenient way of hitting town or to see a particular site.

25

I made the decision to always stick with the white blazes, but not just to "be official." Quite simply, I didn't want to be at a camp fire and have someone say "Wow, did you see that [insert thing here] today" or "Boy oh boy, wasn't that Trail magic awesome?" only to realize that I missed it by taking a blue blaze. Between you and me though, after 2,200 miles, that never once happened.

Someone that "yellow blazes" is someone that chooses to follow the yellow lines of the road, probably by car or bus, and therefore did not do any hiking at all for that portion. When I reached Harpers Ferry, West Virginia, I looked through the photo album and saw a lady claiming to be a Southbounder starting in Maine after me. Somehow she had passed me even though I was going pretty fast and nobody I talked to remembered seeing her journal entries at shelters or meeting her. Randomly throughout the remaining two months of my hike I would talk to people that met her and they all said pretty much the same thing: "she said she was a thru-hiker starting in Maine, but she's apparently putting on weight and doesn't have much to say about the Trail." Finally I found a very reputable source that told me she was yellow blazing and skipping hundreds of miles of trail at a time – he told me that while she says she "started in Maine" she is intentionally being vague because she actually started in Portland, at the airport, and skipped all of the AT in Maine.

The problem here isn't that she was yellow blazing. The problem is that she was telling people she was a thru-hiker, which gives you discounts on lodging, food, and various other perks, when she clearly wasn't. There are free and pay hostels along the Trail that will kick you out if they learn you are planning to do anything less than a thru-hike. I met someone that was kicked out of such a place when they learned he was only hiking 500 miles that year. As it happens, if he planned to hike the whole thing, but fell ill at 500 miles and had to cancel his trip, he would have been allowed to stay. When I asked him about this possibility, he said he couldn't lie and would feel bad taking resources away from thru-hikers that needed it more than him.

Last but not least, what on earth is aqua blazing? There are a few places on the AT where rivers conveniently flow roughly alongside the Trail, such as the Shenandoah River in Virginia and the Housatonic River in Connecticut. Hikers will get off the Trail, head to town and find an outfitter that rents tubes/boats so they can float downstream and connect back up to the Trail. If they don't float their gear with them, they may rely on the outfitter to shuttle it for them.

Did you get any Trail magic?

Is that slang for stepping on bear scat? Are you asking if David Copperfield was thru-hiking too? Would my wife think I was unfaithful if I answered "Yes" to this question? Is it like that bridge crossing scene in *Monty Python and the Holy Grail?*!

Far from it. "Trail magic" is when something that can be considered a treat is left on the trail to be found and used by hikers. This can be beverages, snacks, fruit, donuts, fresh rolls of toilet paper, whatever. Trail magic also happens when you walk through a campground, park, what have you, and someone invites you over to eat all their wonderful food. There are even locals who make it a tradition to come out to the Trail for a specific weekend every year to grill up and provide food to any hiker passing through the area.

The best Trail magic I encountered was in Massachusetts. It consisted of a cooler full of ice, soda and Gatorade sitting next to another cooler full of snack cakes and granola bars (coolers are reasonably resistant to animal intruders and the weather). On two occasions someone left various beverages in cold, shallow streams - if the water level came up, chances are they'd end up miles downstream. Usually there's a garbage bag

Delicious Trail magic! Drinks, snacks, chips and a garbage bag!

nearby for when you're done, but it's also there so you can also put your own garbage in.

Trail magic is not officially sanctioned by the managers of the AT and in fact is somewhat discouraged. It's a tough line for them to walk. On the one hand it is basically littering, even more so when the person leaving out the treats never returns for the garbage and it can attract animals of all sizes and lead to unsafe health and safety situations. On the other hand, were it not for people leaving out large caches of water at road crossings in the south to combat the drought conditions, I'm sure there would have been some medical emergencies from dehydration.

The people that leave Trail magic are called Trail Angels, and this is just one of the reasons they get that name. Trail Angels are also people that go out of their way to help out a hiker. This can be in the form of transportation, lodging, food, etc. Doing something to help out a hiker when they could have just as easily turned away earns them a nickname of Trail Angel.

Trail Angels are often people that once hiked the AT or have had a lifelong dream of hiking it but feel they never will. In essence they want to give something to the Trail and vicariously be a part of it. And, of course, sometimes they're just naturally good people doing a good deed. We love Trail Angels!

Did you ever slack pack?

Slack packing is, in a sense, related to aqua or yellow blazing. You, the reader, may have actually done it without even knowing it. The concept is that you hike while your backpack doesn't. This commonly happens when you find a local that says "Hey, you can stay at my place, I'll drive you to the trailhead in the morning and pick you up at this other trailhead and bring you back home."

There are also businesses or thrifty locals that you can pay to slack pack you - some can operate over very vast ranges. It's fairly common and I've never heard of anyone being swindled.

I took it as a matter of pride to hike every mile with all my gear and only slack packed once in very special circumstances. Three friends drove over to Vermont from New York to hike up and over Bromley Mountain Ski Resort with me and I let them convince me to leave my pack in the car for the five or so miles. Am I ashamed? No!

If you have enough money, you can even slack pack the 100 Mile Wilderness. For the few nights I stayed in Monson, Maine, just outside the 100 Mile Wilderness, there was a retired gentleman that was not prepared at all for a thru-hike. After a few false starts - turned away by the park rangers who sensed he was out of his element - he ended up paying the hostel owners to navigate the multitude of logging roads to the various trailheads each day to slack pack him. I imagine it cost him several hundred dollars.

Extreme adventure?

I was once in a friendly debate with another Southbounder about whether or not I would call the AT experience "extreme" or "hardcore." To me, walking 2,200 miles wasn't extreme, but I conceded that to run it or do it naked would be.

No, the Appalachian Trail isn't extreme in the sense that you will be fighting off monkeys, cutting down trees for shelter, or building rafts to ford raging rivers. But, yes, it is extreme in the sense that it's not something most people choose to do.

I honestly was hoping for some extreme adventure. Maybe a forest fire or landslide blocking my way; a river requiring me to swim and somehow haul my pack over on a rope; an injured leg forcing me to hobble to a road while being tracked by a mountain lion. Something to make me feel alive, but in the end the AT simply felt to me like one long walk in a local park. If, for some reason, I was unable to continue, I could simply sit down and wait a few hours for someone to inevitably walk past and then perhaps a day or two for them to get help to me - all the while I could just relax in my hammock and eat from my food bag.

I'm sure there are others who feel that simply the 2,200 miles alone makes it an extreme adventure, but I never really felt boredom or loneliness, and the only reason I was glad to be done was so that I could move on to something better.

Looking ready for adventure atop a mountain in Maine.

I had a compass with me simply because, on more than one occasion, I needed the mirror it came with to help remove dirt or a bug from my eye, but if the direction arrow was broken it would have made no difference.

I think I'll split the difference and take the stance that it was an "extreme experience" but not an "extreme adventure."

Gosh, isn't it scary? Dangerous?

People these days are so afraid of the wild that it makes me sad. I can't blame it on the media, or horror movies, or parents, because the thing is, it seems like we've always been afraid. When Europeans came to North America they saw the forests, reaching off into forever, full of sounds and animals they'd never known, so they just cut everything down and killed anything that moved. Classic fairy tales are based on this concept and play on society's fear of the unknown and often conjure up monsters within the woods. It's simply human nature to be afraid of the unfamiliar.

I'm as much a victim of this as anyone. I grew up in civilization; I wasn't exposed much to the outdoors and camping with the Boy Scouts meant the car was always nearby. It took about a month of hiking on the

AT before my mind adjusted to the noises at night and allowed me to sleep soundly. Was that a bear??!??! Ah, no, just a squirrel. Was THAT a bear?!?!? Nope, just a deer. That??? A chipmunk. And after 2,200 miles you realize you never once heard a bear in the woods at night.

In Maine's 100 Mile Wilderness, with my friend Adam, I awoke to strange noises all around us. "Psst, Adam, do you hear that?" I call out across the camp trying to hide my concern. Without a care in the world he calmly replies "stupid squirrels." From that moment on, whenever I heard a strange sound at night I would tell myself "stupid squirrels" and imagine Adam sleeping soundly through it all.

These days with relatively so little wild left around the AT, I am shocked that we still feel this way. I'm not shocked that people are wary or apprehensive - it takes a while to get used to the outdoors just as it takes a while to get used to city noises - but I'm shocked by the people who are quite literally afraid. They can be so fearful that they can't even fathom the concept or won't even give it a try. It probably borders on phobia and to me it is a shame. One lady in her 60's stopped on her way inside a grocery store in Pearisburg, Virginia to talk to me.

"Are you doing the Trail?" she asked.

"Yes, I'm heading south."

"Are you alone???"

"Pretty much, yeah" I reply, "but I see lots of people every day."

"Well, my son wanted to do the Trail years ago and I put my foot down! That's simply too dangerous and I wouldn't have it" she said very proudly and walked away with her head held high.

Poor guy. I like to believe that he still did the Trail but told his mom that work was really busy so that's why he didn't answer the phone for five months.

The funny thing is that most of the people telling me about the perceived dangers of the Trail were doing so in exactly the wrong situations. For example, a father with his family was telling his kids in a low and serious voice just how hard the hike must be for me. "Kids, this man is walking over TWO thousand miles all by himself! He carries everything he needs in that backpack and has to know things like First Aid in case something happens to him." He then turns to me to add, "Isn't it scary to be so far from civilization?" On the inside I'm laughing at the irony as I sit on a restaurant porch eating an ice cream and slurping a milk shake. With a smile I reply, "It's not all that remote, if you consider I can buy ice cream like this every few days" and we all chuckle.

Plenty of sources have commented on how, statistically speaking, given the number of people and acreage, the Trail is safer than any town in America. Even so, I read debates about whether one should carry a firearm for protection (from humans as well as animals), and I even met a hiker who started with a handgun simply to placate her family. I once passed a couple that appeared to just be out for the weekend and the man had a gun in a shoulder holster. Most casual hikers will probably need years of experience before they feel comfortable enough to leave the gun behind, but my impression is that it takes only a week or two for thru-hikers to come to their senses.

Just use your head and you'll be fine. If you're talking to someone that you don't think you can trust, don't tell them your life story. It's also a good idea to be vague about where you're going. Rather than "I'm staying at Cloudkill Shelter tonight, you know, that remote shelter where hardly anybody ever goes" simply say "I tend to hike until I get tired, I'm not sure where I'll end up." This is especially important in towns or near roads where you're more likely to come in contact with "creepy types." When coming to a road crossing, perhaps you'll want to wait until you can cross without being seen by passing motorists. Don't set up camp immediately, wait to see who else is staying there, and if you don't feel safe then, you can always leave and find something better.

Did you take any time off?

It is fairly common for hikers to take time off now and then. These are days when you hike zero miles, and are therefore called "zero days." Zero days can happen in a town or on the AT, and can be planned or spontaneous. It is often for mental or physical health reasons, and very often involves family or friends.

One week into my hike, when I hit Monson, Maine, just outside of the 100 Mile Wilderness, I said goodbye to Adam, and hello to one zero day. I felt it was necessary to help kick-start the healing of my injured Achilles tendon. During this time I visited a nearby outfitter, enjoyed restaurant cooking, helped cook a family-style meal for the 15 or so hikers staying in the hostel, and talked at length with all the Northbounders.

About a month after leaving Monson, Maine, I spent the day hiking once again with Adam, but this time we were joined by his wife and her family. They drove me over to New York, where I spent a few days visiting with Adam's family, my family and my wife. During this time, I was happy to let them take me out to lunch or dinner because every meal ended with them passing me their plates so I could scrape them clean. I fondly remember finishing a few plates at a casual Mexican restaurant one night, and a few more at a formal restaurant the next. I could barely restrain myself from asking the tables around us for their leftovers.

One more month into the hike, I was picked up in Maryland by my wife, to spend six days at home in Washington, DC. Now, two and a half months in to the hike, having lost 20 pounds of body fat and muscle between Maryland and Maine, food was all I could think about. I would wake up each morning, eat breakfast then head to the corner store for a pint of ice cream. I would eat a hearty lunch and then go searching for a pint of ice cream. Sometime between dinner and bedtime I would head to the corner store for another pint or two. My wife would laugh at me, not because I enjoyed eating all this ice cream, but because I needed as many calories and as much fat that I could get my hands on.

The Daleville and Troutvile exit on Interstate 81 in central Virginia is a busy truck stop with plenty of motels, strip malls and four lane roads. Not generally thought of as a hiker heaven. However, the outfitter there is top notch, and more importantly, there is a grocery store and BBQ restaurant walking distance from the motel. I stayed two nights there just so I could enjoy that BBQ!

When I hit the southern border of Virginia a month later, I took four days off to attend a conference in Gettysburg, Pennsylvania. The conference was the annual "Gathering," thrown by the Appalachian Long Distance

Hikers Association. It gave me a great opportunity to learn more about the AT, other thru-hikers, other trails, and spend more time visiting the wife. When I left DC, my plan was to eat more as I hiked in order to regain lost weight or at least maintain what I still had. I think the plan worked, because I have fewer food-related memories from my time in Gettysburg.

5. A Walk in New Hampshire

The first and best view I would have of Mount Washington. Rain and clouds would obstruct the view for most of my time in the Whites.

Length:	161 miles	259 km
Max Elevation:	6,288 feet	1,917 m
Min Elevation:	400 feet	122 m
My First Day:	July 4	
My Last Day	July 16	

What's it like?

New Hampshire is known for its Presidential Range inside the White Mountains (or the Whites), both sharing the glorious Mount Washington. Thru-hikers heading south look forward to New Hampshire, because everything after it is relatively easy; while hikers heading north see it as the start of relatively hard hiking.

When you reflect on your time spent in the state, all you seem to remember are the 117 miles you hiked in the Whites. The remaining 44 miles just tend to blur into Vermont and you have to dig deep to remember what they were like.

It's easy to remember the Whites not only because of their sheer size and magnitude, but because they're surrounded by legend, myth, and tales from hikers about their daunting nature. To hike to the Whites from Georgia, they are a stark contrast to anything you'd seen before, whereas I saw them simply as an amped up version of Maine.

It is no small feat to go from 400 feet to more than 6,000, but at least you do it gradually or in shorter bursts. I wish I could say that all the views were phenomenal (as they are supposed to be), but most of my time was spent in a cloud bank. Just days before I entered the White Mountains, in early July, an inch of snow fell on Mount Washington (which can happen any time of the year). Because of their placement on the continent, they can experience tornado force winds, rain, snow, fog, virtually any kind of weather at any time of year.

For a few brief hours, the sky did clear up just below the summit of Mount Washington while spending the night at the Lake of the Clouds Hut, affording me a chance to take a few photos (one of which won me an award in an "outdoor grandeur" photo contest!).

And that's the beauty of these mountains, that in less than an hour they can go from 50 feet visibility, 40 mph winds with driving rain and near freezing temperatures, to breathtakingly clear and grandiose.

At the end of a long day of hiking, I needed to get to the other end of Franconia Ridge, the second expanse of ridge line above tree line in the Whites, before the sun went down. Hiking in a cloud bank, I was anxious to be done with the ridge and get to my camp ground. I knew as I left the tree line and entered the exposed ridge that I had several miles and several mini summits to go before returning to the trees. However, the lack of visibility prevented me from seeing even the first summit. I kept wondering where the first one was, or if I was on the first one, or already past the first one, and then the clouds would part and I'd see, way off in the distance, what was quite obviously a summit and then the clouds would return. This process repeated for the full length

Walking along Franconia Ridge in the Whites.

of the ridge – I would wonder where the next summit was or if I was on it, and then eerily the clouds would lift and I'd have my answer.

When I reached the campground, the caretaker informed me that none of the available tent platforms were any good for hammocks, but that if I did want to stay (and use the bear boxes, privy and spring water), he suggested a spot that other hammock hangers had used in the past. I was led down a side trail to a side trail and was essentially in the middle of nowhere far from the noises of camp. When it came time to lock my food in the camp's bear box, I strapped on my headlamp and began the two minute walk. After 10 feet, I turned around and through the thick fog I could barely make out the reflective guy lines hanging from my rain fly. At 15 feet I could only see them because I knew where to look. At 20 feet my camp was swallowed completely by the fog and dark of night. The trail through the maze of trees I had to follow was hardly ever used and so it was difficult to make out even during the day. Rather than get lost in the cold, dense New Hampshire forest, I opted to return to camp and hang my food directly above my hammock – this was the only place I could see a branch high enough and I comically figured a bear might be confused by the hammock hanging in between him and the food.

The ups and downs can be very steep and long, placing a heavy burden on the knees, which is why many hikers will travel with less food and make up for it by eating and sheltering at the Huts (more about this later). Travelers who haven't learned to travel light by the time they hit New Hampshire are in for a rude awakening.

The nicest part about being in the Whites is mosquitoes and black flies really aren't a factor due to the elevation, cold temperatures, and wind. There were a few times I camped in sheltered valley regions which could easily have been infested, but it was pouring rain so I'll never know.

On the Vermont border, in Hanover, New Hampshire, you will find Dartmouth College. What I like about Hanover is that the Trail goes down Main Street and as such there are white blazes on telephone poles and street signs. There was a time when the outing club would shelter hikers on campus, but in 2007 that was abolished for student safety reasons. You will probably need a car to take you to one of the few motels just outside of town if you need lodging.

A few highlights

It's cliché to say Mount Washington, the Presidential Range and Franconia Ridge are the highlights, so you'll just have to trust me that they're all worth visiting (and all very accessible by car).

Apart from the obvious, there is one place that stands out for a few reasons: Mount Moosilauke (*moo sill aw key*). Moosilauke is a less visited mountain, because it is overshadowed by the rest of the range. However, it is one heck of a great hike. The mountain summit is void of trees, so you get a stunning 360 degree view. You can also see the crumbled remains of stone buildings - serving as a reminder of the various structures that stood at the top many years ago. The Appalachian Trail crosses Route 112 and joins the Beaver Brook Trail taking you up to Mount Moosilauke. But it won't be an easy hike. Like its White Mountain brethren, the trail is very steep; unlike its brethren it's not exactly a hard rock surface. Beaver Brook Trail is densely forested and the ground is loose soil, root and rock. Just days before my arrival, heavy rains caused several sections of trail to wash out and many trees were lying sideways. Sections of trail were entirely missing, leaving only portions of stone steps as evidence that a trail once existed. Caution tape was woven throughout the landscape while rebar (there to hold lumber or stones in place) was left embedded in the ground as a reminder.

Zealand Falls flowing furiously - a short distance from the Zealand Falls Hut.

6. Introspection

Why!?!?!

Why I hiked the AT is perhaps the most common question and yet I still don't have an answer I fully believe. Nonetheless, I trained myself to be quick with a response that would please the listener and leave me free to continue my trek. Since my reasons aren't terribly inspirational, I'll first rely on the various stories I picked up along the way to answer this question.

One story told to me by the Mayor of Unionville, New York was about two guys hiking the Trail because it was a dream of their good friend who died the year before and this was their way of honoring him.

Then there was a tale about a lady hiking to regain her faith in humanity in the aftermath of her military service. The Trail definitely has the power to heal scars like that.

My less motivational responses included but were not limited to:

- I'm an outdoors person that was working in a cube far too much, and I decided I needed a swift kick to the head to get some wilderness back in me.
- It's something I've wanted to do for a long time (since reading Bryson's book!) and the timing was finally right.
- I've always enjoyed pushing myself and this would be a good test.

But the answer I believed in most was that I simply wanted to prove that, if I had to, it was possible for me to walk from one corner of the country to the other. Simple and honest. Some people want to hear something more profound, a spiritual drive of some kind, so for them I might add in something about helping to convince society that they need not rely so much on cars and the like.

Whatever floats your sandal. There are as many reasons for hiking the AT as there are people hiking it. Lose weight, get in shape, try something different, walk in a relative's footsteps, or as a way to fill in some down time in your life.

Had you done anything like this before?

Had I done anything that had mentally or physically prepared me for this? How did I know what equipment to bring? Did I have any idea what I was in for?

To some extent I did know what I was getting in to. While I hadn't done anything quite like this, I did grow up camping with the Boy Scouts. Yes, most of it was car camping, but on two separate occasions I was able to go to a large private park in New Mexico for five- and seven-day backpacking trips. When I was old enough to drive, a friend and I would head up to the Adirondack Mountains in New York for backpacking weekends. For the most part, these were well planned and heavily geared trips - my pack was nowhere near light and nimble.

From 15 years old to 30, I pretty much always used the same camping gear. It was big, heavy, and built to last a lifetime. I used this gear to take a 40 mile winter hike on the C&O Canal along the Potomac River with my friend Adam and again when we decided to bicycle all 184 miles of it.

It was from this C&O Canal bike trip that I learned about bicycle camping, which lead to my undertaking of a 636 mile, seven day bike trip around the mountains, lakes and cow pastures of New York. At this point I was officially hooked on solo camping and long-distance adventure but certainly didn't think that a year and a half later I'd be tackling the AT.

All my experiences had taught me that potable (safe for consumption) water didn't have to be crystal clear, that I could wear the same set of clothes for an indefinite period of time, that hiking in the rain was a free shower AND Laundromat, and that lightning storms were fun.

I understood the importance of lightweight and minimal gear, but I didn't realize how out-of-date my equipment was. While researching the AT, I saw just how light and compact everything had become and decided it was time to upgrade my closet.

Would you do it again?

It's such a positive experience that, for many people, lifelong friendships, memories, and lifestyle changes can result. It's no wonder that so many people dream of doing it again - and a large number will hike it repeatedly.

During my hike and in the months after, my response was always "No. I loved the experience but I think there are other trails better suited to me." A year later, the nostalgia takes over and my response becomes "No. Well, maybe, but this time in a different direction or at a different time of year."

A full TWO years later and I'm so anxious to hike ANY long distance trail that I'd even consider hiking the AT with a crowd of Northbounders! It becomes part of you and for better or for worse will most likely define who you are for the rest of your life. "This is Ken, our new employee, he hiked the Appalachian Trail" or "Ken, I was looking to take the family camping. Did I hear that you do a lot of hiking?" I am now "that person" in the office, the one people come to for outdoors advice, and Heaven help the person that asks me a question about the AT because I'll start talking and never shut up.

In case you haven't figured it out yet, I was expecting the Trail to be less populated and more remote. I did, however, love the freedom it afforded me. I had no schedules, no deadlines, and I rarely had to plan anything ahead of time. I thrived on the constant physical exertion, and even the mindless monotony. The outdoors were far superior to the urban jungle, and I truly loved being surrounded by so much of it.

I do often wonder what the Trail would be like if I hiked it out-of-season; leaving from Maine in September or from Georgia in January. Or maybe I would simply bounce around and see the places I missed most.

Don't get me wrong, hiking the Appalachian Trail was absolutely the right decision and I wouldn't take it back even if I could. If I was given the choice of hiking the Pacific Crest Trail or the Appalachian Trail in 2007, I would still be writing this book. It was the perfect first step for what I hope will be a long life of long-distance adventures.

I met a lot of ex-thru-hikers and was surprised to hear them recount their favorite memories... of bars, parties, beer, and friends. It seemed that if "woods," "wildlife," or "isolation" were to come up in the conversation it would be only a small part. It's not to say that they weren't important, but probably with four to six months of trees, mountains, streams and rocks, you tend to focus on other things. The human interaction is what seems to set the AT apart from many other long-distance trails, and therefore it also draws a lot of people looking for just that sort of thing. I certainly miss the friends I made on the trail or in towns and would love to see them again, so I understand the feeling. I, however, wanted to commune with nature, not my fellow man.

Doesn't anybody miss you?

I understood early on that I needed to make sure my AT experience wasn't a selfish one. Be it friends, family, or neighbors, I didn't want anyone to feel abandoned. Even so, I'm sure at least my wife missed me.

I tried my best to make sure people wouldn't miss me by writing up a two-sided, triple-fold pamphlet and mailing or delivering it to every-

Saying goodbye to my wife at the Maryland border.

one I could think of. This would introduce them to the Appalachian Trail and how I intended to take it on.

I assembled a team (referred to as my Base Camp) that consisted of my wife, my friend Adam and his wife Sara. I made sure to keep them abreast of my progress so that they could distribute the information and, in case of emergency, contact the right people. This was also intended as a support group for my wife, even if she didn't realize it, to make my absence more tolerable should that be an issue.

Base Camp was responsible for maintaining my website (which I will discuss shortly) and had access to my e-mail accounts as well as permission to send out email updates should I request they do so. And because I was trying to cut off my ties with technology, my Base Camp communications were few and my communications with anyone outside of those three people were even fewer.

Not-so-secretly I was hoping the AT would train my friends and family to be accustomed to my absence so that if and when I took on far more remote trails like the Pacific Crest or Continental Divide they wouldn't worry so much.

So, yes, I was missed, but I'd like to think that I did a reasonable job ensuring that nobody went crazy with worry or fear. I'd like to believe that while my hike was solitary, my journey was shared.

The simple truth is that there are plenty of opportunities to find internet access, a pay phone, a free phone or reception for your cell phone, not to mention sending postcards, letters or packages. If you are concerned about losing touch with people you care about, there are ways to make the separation more tolerable.

Are you alone?

They say that Southbounders are introverts who prefer to keep to themselves and make the AT into a quiet and humbling experience. That was certainly the case for me.

But the question is quite poorly worded. Yes, I do NOT have a hiking partner; I am basically hiking the AT alone. No, I am not actually alone, because the trail often feels busier than a shopping mall on Black Friday and you have to work pretty hard to find yourself away from people.

In the first month, it was nearly impossible to find solitude as there

I wasn't alone when I started. In the background is Adam, before he became part of my Base Camp.

were simply too many Northbounders, weekenders, section-hikers, Boy

Scouts, Girl Scouts, Outward Bound groups, and on and on. I wasn't walking with anyone per se, but every shelter, campground or mountain top seemed to be occupied.

From Katahdin to New York the only time I think I was alone at a camp/shelter was the one just south of Stratton, Maine in a cold rain a short distance down a side trail to the Crocker Cirque Campsite. A few times I came close when hikers opted to pitch their tents further in to the woods for a better view or flatter location and were thus out of sight.

If I truly did want to camp by myself I didn't have to stay in shelters or at camp sites, but I liked having a nearby water source and privy. Later on, in the south, when water was rarely running at a shelter, I frequently hung my hammock in random locations on the side of the trail (or if I found a nice vista!) and camped alone. By then, too, I was content with digging my own "cat hole" to substitute for a privy.

Most of the Southbounders I knew liked hiking alone but camping with people. For me it entirely depended on who I was with. In Maine, I enjoyed hiking alone and camping with Brit and Smoky. From New Hampshire to New York, I hiked alone and didn't camp with another Southbounder - except for spending two consecutive nights with Thorny in Vermont. With Brit, Smoky, and Thorny we would say goodbye in the morning and say hello at camp - occasionally meeting at a snack stop. Thorny was, in fact, the last Southbounder I saw until I caught up with Lady and the Tramp (a lady traveling with her dog), just before the New Jersey border.

When I ran in to Lady, she was walking with her cousin for a week. For the most part, the three of us not only camped together but we also hiked together. Her cousin was eager for conversation (the monotony was getting to her) and I was happy to oblige - after all, I had a lot to talk about after 350 miles without another Southbounder, and Lady and I had met a lot of the same people early on. So I slowed my pace and miles-per-day and we had a fun time talking and walking. Once her cousin left us, I found that Lady and I had a very similar level of endurance and our daily mileage goals were about equal.

When we hit Delaware Water Gap, Pennsylvania, she went to spend the night with family and planned on a late start the following day, while I stayed in town and intended for an early start. As it happens, I was forced to stay in town longer in order to wait for the Post Office to open and as I was finally making my way up the road to the trailhead a car drove by and dropped Lady off 15 feet ahead of me - her plans changed and she got an early start. Having been reunited, Lady, Tramp and I tramped along and shared stories and food for all of Pennsylvania.

Near the end of Pennsylvania, the three of us caught up to Mr. Wiffle, another Southbounder, who would end up walking and camping with us for about a week. A younger fellow of tall and thin proportions, his nickname came from the yellow plastic wiffle ball bat he carried at the start of the Trail.

When Lady left the Trail again, I happened to take seven days off and the first morning back on the Trail I had Brit, Smoky, Quasi, and Sweet Tea (all of whom I'd known from Maine or New Hampshire) practically walk into me as I was taking down camp. When I opened the door to exit the privy, I looked up to see a surprised Smoky waiting with toilet paper in hand - I too was shocked. The next few days we all spent together, hiking and relaxing in Harpers Ferry, West Virginia. I had hoped we could continue as a group, but they were exhausted and needed more time off. At this time, Lady was dropped off in town and since we were both anxious to keep hiking she and I decided to leave them behind so we could tackle Virginia. A few days later in Front Royal, Virginia, I said goodbye to Lady once again and for the last time as she went off, once again, to visit family.

From Front Royal, Virginia it's 955 miles to Springer Mountain in Georgia and in that time I only saw one other Southbounder. I almost always had a good idea of who was behind me during this last, long stretch, and a great idea of who was ahead. If I was ever lonely I COULD have increased my pace to catch Mr. Wiffle or Chilly who were only 1-4 days ahead, or slow down and wait 1-4 days for Fiesta, Siesta, Quasi, Stoker, Sweet Tea, Brit, Smoky, Ranger or Yellowbird to catch me.

This is how the Trail works. People will come and go and you never have to be alone if you don't want to. I recall only one three day period (somewhere in Virginia) where I didn't even see another person, period. Cars and roads, yes, but three days without a day-hiker, weekender, sectioner or thru-hiker. All the same, if I had just stopped for a few hours, I'm sure someone would have happened upon me.

Weren't you bored?

It's no surprise that the AT is considered more of a mental challenge than a physical one, especially when you take into account the frequency with which I was asked if I was ever bored. Boredom is a big factor and encompasses a lot more than just being fidgety. It's a mental attitude that is so strong it forces many to leave the AT for good, even when their physical state is perfect.

A lot of hikers carry some form of music and/or reading material. To save weight I initially opted for neither, and gradually realized I simply didn't desire the distraction. I spent my days thinking, singing songs I knew, singing songs I didn't know and making up songs. I also spent a lot of time doing nothing - in a sort of mindless trance. A few times I wondered if I'd enjoy a portable radio or mp3 player but figured that would cheapen the experience for me. It was bad enough I was carrying a cell phone (used sparingly); listening to music I feared would pull me away from what little wilderness there was.

I usually found amusement in simple things, like this unrelenting wind in Maine!

I did get savvy once and asked Adam's father-in-law to periodically send me clippings from newspapers and magazines rather than carrying whole books. Unfortunately I only did this once and found that I simply didn't know far enough in advance where my next mail stops would be. But I liked the idea and would definitely ask for the same service on any future trips.

Unfortunately, there's only so much one can do to fight off boredom if it comes knocking. Perhaps Northbounders have it easier because there are so many more people around them - and perhaps that's why it seems like a Northbounder's experience focuses so much more on towns. To enjoy a solo thru-hike, you simply must enjoy spending time with yourself. It certainly helps.

Did you ever want to quit?

There were maybe only five days when I wanted to quit, and each one of those days followed on the heels of a bad night's sleep. Once I realized that these feelings were brought on by sleep deprivation, I was able to look past it and ignore future occurrences. At the same time, I became more adept at finding places to sleep where I wouldn't be dealing with snoring (oh my God, the snoring!!!), like by avoiding busy shelters or bunk houses.

In the first two months, I also had a few instances of what I've decided to call "wandering feet." Times when I would come in contact with bicyclists and feel a very strong desire to switch into my cycling shoes and just start riding to the Pacific, leaving the Trail far behind. It's probably worth noting that, in the months before my decision to hike the AT, I was strongly considering a bicycle trip across country, so forgive me if I admit that while hiking I often daydreamed of traveling 100 miles in a day at a pace that prevented mosquitoes from catching me.

But I was fortunate in that I never had [significant] health problems, I never became [too] ill, my finances held up, my taste for trail food never waned and the boredom never set in. I also understood that, deep down, even if I wanted to quit, I would never accept anything less than completing the full length of the Trail. With that knowledge, my subconscious might have decided not to waste its energy on filling my head with desires to quit.

My Pez dispenser wouldn't let me quit, even if I wanted to! In Maine I started eating yogurt to help stay healthy.

There's also a funny bi-polar phenomena on the AT where people manage to convince themselves to prematurely return home but end up returning to the Trail weeks later. On the AT they're miserable and desperate to put the experience behind them, but after a week or two of "real life" an amazingly strong desire to put the backpack back on surfaces that they can't shake. One lady I ran into had left the Trail three times because she was so unhappy, and each time after a week she'd start missing it so much that she just had to come back and continue.

Even hikers that finish the AT will experience this and find it hard not to start a new hike right away. This is probably why a lot of people will "yo-yo" the Trail - meaning to go from Maine to Georgia to Maine and vice versa.

7. A Walk in Vermont

Remnants of an old ski lift on top of Bromley Mountain Ski Resort in Vermont.

Length:	150 miles	259 km
Max Elevation:	4,010 feet	1,222 m
Min Elevation:	400 feet	122 m
My First Day:	July 16	
My Last Day:	July 27	

What's it like?

Mosquitoes, mud, roots, and ski slopes. That's what quickly comes to mind, however trite it may sound. Truth be told, it's at least one bullet point more than Massachusetts.

The AT in Vermont isn't as beautiful as its New Hampshire neighbor, but it is one of the more interesting sections. On two separate occasions you will be walking on ski slopes, under chair lifts, and enjoying spectacular summer time views from these famous winter recreation areas. I remember finely crafted shelters complete with handicapped accessible outhouses, shelters with views of the valley, and the wonderful smell of the woods drying out after heavy rains.

But mostly I remember vaulting over pits of mud while trying not to slip on tree roots. Oh, and that one campsite on top of a hill with a firing range at the base, probably more than a mile away but still sounding awfully close.

The Long Trail is an historic 273 mile long trail (the first long-distance trail in the US) running the length of Vermont, and for 100 miles the AT shares the same ground. It's a mental milestone when you finally hit the Long Trail because it marks the moment when the AT decisively heads south and won't be turning west until you reach the bottom of Connecticut. Being on the Long Trail somehow feels more historic even though the look and feel of the trail hasn't really changed.

Some will say that Vermont is the least friendly state; that everyone drives BMW's and Audi's and doesn't care one lick for hikers. Yes, I will admit that Vermont does seem to possess more luxury vehicles than any other state, and I never found the folks in town to be too interested in what I was doing, or giving me a ride, or even saying "Hi," but I wouldn't say they were unfriendly. Vermont simply seems cautious and at worst maybe just uninterested – certainly not malicious. And besides, I'm willing to blame it all on the fact that by the time thru-hikers hit Vermont they can be quite smelly, dirty and unkempt.

The woods themselves have a unique magic to them. There were two occasions where I can remember hiking through very tall, very straight,

A very uniform, tight growth of trees in Vermont.

stands of perhaps 30 year old pine trees. They were in an almost perfect grid-like pattern, I had to believe they were planted by hand. A local told me that most likely they were one of the areas planted by airplane and that without any competition from other vegetation they were allowed to grow with this symmetrical spacing.

Vermont is also home to some comedically inclined trail crews, as evidenced by the privies. There was one (named Cloudland) that was six sided, four feet across, a roof to match, and the top half of each wall (including the door) was screened in. Sitting down on the toilet your head and shoulders would be visible from all sides but at least there was good ventilation. Even more ventilated was the privy that was placed on the top of a small flight of steps, in real throne-like fashion, with a roof supported by pillars – no walls at all.

A few highlights

Hiking on ski resorts like Killington and Bromley Mountain is a neat feeling. You get great views of the surrounding Green Mountain National Forest and can see all the tiny little towns in the distance. Buildings are in a summer-time hibernation and waiting for the snow to fall so they can come back to life and the chairs and lift cables sway in the breeze. Being that they are also ski resorts, these mountains are easily accessible for day hikes.

My most positive memory from Vermont is the smell of the trees. On occasions when the sun made an appearance, the aroma of drying birch and pine trees would fill the nostrils and cleanse the system.

After hiking for weeks in pouring rain, I reached The Inn at Long Trail on Route 4 near Killington completely soaked through and on the verge of shivering. I'm sure the inn is perfectly wonderful any time of year, but it was absolutely Heaven on earth for me at that time. I filled up at the pub and dried out my clothes with the help of some newspaper from the recycling bin.

The unique Cloudland privy.

8. Perspectives

Why southbound? Which way is better?

Like a baby's diaper, this topic is loaded. The direction you go really depends on the type of person you are and your schedule. Me? I went south primarily because I couldn't start until June. When I was on the Trail I realized that it was the perfect direction for me because it meant more solitude and less noise.

But why else? Apart from population control, there's a multitude of reasons for choosing one direction over the other. Northbounders tend to "walk with spring" and find their way highlighted with wildflowers, cheerful animals, berries, high water levels and flowing springs. They have more Trail magic, more support from towns and festivals along the way. Sounds great, right? What about more biting bugs and the financially annoying task of needing both cold and warm weather gear? Southbounders generally experience less extreme temperatures and, in exchange for wildflowers, we get fall foliage in the Smoky Mountains!

There are books and websites devoted to this conversation; I'm not even scratching the surface. Keep in mind that no matter which way is better or easier, the success rate is still around 10-20%.

Thru versus section?

I was asked once by a friend if there was any caste structure placed upon hikers - if, for example, thru-hikers looked down on section-hikers. Well, there is and there isn't. In this case the basic premise is that at the top of the "self-importance ladder" would be the thru-hikers, followed by flip-floppers (those who hike part of the AT in one direction and the rest of it in the other), then section-hikers, then vacationers, then day-hikers.

While I'm sure there are a good number of hikers at each step that do feel they are more important than those beneath them, that's not the point I want to raise. Yes, on many occasions I did have a day-hiker make the comment "I'm surprised you stopped to talk, most thru-hikers think they're too important" or conversely when I kept my head down and kept walking: "Hey I saw you on the trail last week but you just blew right by without saying hello." It's because of the latter that many casual hikers might feel that I had an attitude and looked down upon them.

The truth is a bit simpler and, at least for me, somewhat redeeming. Sometimes I don't have time to stop to talk to every person I meet! Run the numbers and you'll see that I can sometimes pass 50 people a day and sometimes just making eye contact is enough to spark up a 10 minute conversation - there's not enough time in my day for that. Indeed, there were many hikers who made these distractions part of their hike, but that wasn't in my game plan. If the weather was questionable, or there was a shelter/view I really wanted to get to that day, or I was close to town and desperate for real food, I would probably not want to stop to chat if it meant jeopardizing those plans.

My decision to stop was often predicated on just how beneficial I thought the conversation might be. If water sources are a concern, I'm more likely to get that info from a thru-hiker or even a section-hiker, so if you look like a day-hiker, I'm likely to give you the look that says "Hi, nice day, but please don't stop me." On the flip side, if I'm curious about what a town has to offer, I might want to talk with a day-hiker who is more likely to be a local. These kinds of things go through my head, and I don't think you can avoid operating that way when you're walking for four months, lest it turn in to six.

Starting in mid-June in Maine meant that I immediately started seeing Northbounders on the tail end of their journey - be it in shelter registers or face-to-face (the last one I saw was near Palmerton, Pennsylvania). In those early days, information seemed like such an important factor in any meeting of hikers that virtually every conversation would revolve around what to expect of the days and months ahead. What shelters are "sweet," which hostels are free, where to get the best milk shake, where you might be able to "do the big miles."

As time went by, I began to think all Nobo's were liars - either intentionally or accidentally, it didn't matter - and by Vermont I either stopped asking or stopped listening. Many Sobo's shared this sentiment and it would become a topic of conversation whenever a group of us got together. I'm sure the Nobo's felt the same way about us.

The shame of it is that it took me until Virginia to figure everything out. It's all about perspective and none of us were exactly lying, we simply didn't understand how the Trail changes over time.

Perspective: bears in New Jersey

It seemed that every Nobo in New England told me I'd see bears at every shelter in New Jersey - that they'd calmly come to the shelter to steal food. That I'd see them in Connecticut all along the trail and they wouldn't be afraid of humans.

Why is it, then, that I never saw those bears? I walk quietly, I don't even use noisy hiking poles and my food bag was very breathable and therefore should put off quite the aroma. Well, at some point in a hotel in Virginia, watching the Discovery Channel, I learned that bears have a phenomenal memory when it comes to food. They remember almost to the day when they can find edibles at a specific location and will come back, even years later, to that very spot at that time of year. This helps them to easily find berries, acorns, fish and even hiker food once they know where it is. I'm willing to bet that the Nobo's weren't lying, but since they travel in such large numbers the bears now associate that time of the year with easy food. By the time us Sobo's hit New Jersey, the hiker season is over and the bears have moved on to other sources.

Perspective: ticks in the south

I heard stories about hikers removing up to 20 ticks a day from their skin and clothing in Shenandoah National Park, Virginia. I'd been told to expect ticks all over the south where the grasses are more abundant. I even ran into several hikers diagnosed with Lyme disease who were waiting for a bus to take them home. The few Southbounders I had come to know were all concerned about ticks and were not looking forward to Virginia. Maybe I was just lucky, but on the entire trail I only noticed ticks on two separate occasions, both in Shenandoah National Park in Virginia, and neither time were there more than 10 on me. At the same time, I never once saw a tick capable of carrying the disease - I only saw larval (or stage one) ticks who have yet to bite into another living thing. I began to think that Northbounders simply didn't know what a tick looked like or that they were mistakenly worried about larval ticks.

In the end, I decided that by the time I reached Virginia the trails had been so well traveled that the grasses had been beaten back or even mowed - making it harder to come in contact with the little buggers. I even saw a chart about the lifecycle of ticks and it suggested that stage 2 and 3 ticks (capable of carrying Lyme) were more prevalent in the spring (with the Nobo's) and that during the summer you mostly get stage 1 (with the Sobo's). I might have misunderstood the chart, but it did match my own experience.

Perspective: Trail magic!

This is one you figure out VERY quickly. You're told to expect it and that in the south it's as common as air. In truth, Trail magic is only put out during the northbound season, and the last time I saw Trail magic was at the New York and Connecticut border - and the previous one was just south of Dalton, Massachusetts. In Tennessee, North Carolina and Georgia kind souls had put out water bottles at many road crossings, but this isn't so much about Trail magic as it is about "preventing the death of hikers."

The locals learn when the bulk of hikers are passing through their area and generally don't put out Trail magic any other time of year. The fact that there are so few of us Southbounders means most locals either don't care or don't know when we're passing through. A gentleman in Pennsylvania says to me "You won't make it even if you hurry, you know." I'm towards the front of the southbound pack and making great time so I assume he thinks I'm a Northbounder.

"No, actually, I'm a Southbounder, I have lots of time to get to Georgia," I reply.

Unphased and with certainty he says "Yup, I figured you started in Maine. You should have passed through here months ago."

I'm still confused, knowing how impractical it is to leave Katahdin in June (when the park opens) and hike 1,000 miles to southern Pennsylvania in less than a month. "I'm actually at the front of the pack," I tell him, "there are only seven people in front of me and possibly a few hundred behind".

"No, you guys all passed through months ago, you're at the END of the pack," he says.

If locals can be this confused about when thru-hikers are passing through their region, it's no wonder Trail magic is so sporadic. This is fine because most of the Southbounders I knew were overjoyed to find Trail magic, but we weren't relying on or expecting it.

Perspective: rocks in Pennsylvania

Unfortunately this one has me perplexed. By far the most common complaint about the AT from Northbounders was the rocks in Pennsylvania. You'd swear that, based on how maddeningly agitated they were by Pennsylvania, the rest of the AT must be void of any obstructions. I was even told in no uncertain terms that the trail south of Pennsylvania was flat and smooth, and that the entire state was just rocks. Hikers, books and online

The infamous rocks of Pennsylvania.

forums all had me prepared to see my footwear fall to pieces like Jell-O salad in a wood chipper.

Southbounders would start to worry hundreds of miles in advance, many buying new shoes ahead of time in anticipation of the horror. When I finally hit the Maryland border, I looked back at Pennsylvania and wondered where the rocks were? Yes, there were some isolated instances where there were really sharp and oddly angled rocks covering every inch of ground, and a few places that required patience and careful footing, but nothing that would last long enough to destroy shoes or spirit. My shoes hardly lost any tread; I didn't roll my ankle any more frequently, and those really rocky stretches were over fairly quickly. I have no idea why so many Nobo's would find Pennsylvania worse than any of the previous states, since I found Maryland, Virginia, North Carolina, and Tennessee to be just as rocky.

Perspective: the Trail is flat

Like the rocks in Pennsylvania, this one has my socks in a bunch, although I think MAYBE it has to do with how humans register memories. I was told by many people that once I got to Glencliff, New Hampshire on the southern end of the Whites, the trail would be so flat that I could easily put in 25+ miles a day.

In retrospect there were only a few regions that I'd define as flat for any real length of time: Connecticut, north of Kent, the Pennsylvania ridges and the valley floor around Boiling Springs, and scattered portions of the trail in Virginia. I think that because most of the "flat and easy" sections are in the middle of their journey, by the time the bulk of Nobo's meet up with us they've forgotten what the trail was like and can more readily call to mind the flatness of Connecticut, Pennsylvania and north/central Virginia. Yes, the trail is a lot easier south of Massachusetts, but it's not THAT much easier.

Perspective: regional kindness

This one gets my goat every time (poor goat). Granted, I'm from New York and went to school in Maine, so I'm pretty much from New England and therefore may be biased, but I really tried to look at the regional kindness issue fairly.

I will say that it seems like the south (meaning Southern Virginia, North Carolina, Tennessee and Georgia) is friendlier towards hikers, but I wouldn't go so far as to say any other section is particularly unfriendly. I prefer to say that at worst New England might be indifferent - and besides, it does seem like there are more free hostel-like places to stay between Pennsylvania and Maine.

I do want to raise an important observation on the issue. Most thru-hikers smell, look disheveled and after walking 1,200 miles from Georgia that smell, that look and that attitude are a lot more concentrated. Of course the south appears friendlier; they get to experience cheerful, relatively clean hikers excited about the experience of a lifetime while walking through gorgeous wild flowers! Poor old New England; all they get is dirty, smelly, unkempt hikers who were spoiled by the south and are now complaining about how tired they are and how hilly the terrain is. They're cranky because the bugs bother them, their bank accounts are low, and their friends have quit and gone home. Heck, I was a fellow thru-hiker and that's how *I* perceived most Northbounders - I can't imagine how I'd feel if I were a townsfolk forced to endure that, year after year, for months at a time!

In all likelihood I found New England to be very friendly simply because I looked and acted like a happy, well-rounded individual and the people picked up on this. I also never acquired that "I'm a thru-hiker, I'm entitled to respect and free food/lodging!" mentality that many business owners find tiresome.

Perspective: spring water all the way

In Maine, I learned that a large number of Northbounders didn't EVER filter or treat their water. They claimed that since the start of their journey they always had pristine springs where the ground source was directly accessible. While there's always a raging debate about the need to filter ANY water source, I was more intrigued by the thought that these wonderfully cold and crisp springs I was pulling water from in Maine, would continue the full length of the Trail. These are the folks that write in forums about how wonderful and clean the water is on the AT and that there's no need to even carry a filter or chemical treatment.

Towards the end of the northbound pack, I began hearing about how dry New York, New Jersey and Pennsylvania were and that locals were leaving water jugs on the trail to help out. Springs were indeed drying up, and for most of Pennsylvania through Georgia I'd say they were relatively non-existent - with a few exceptions. Even streams were dry, forcing me to pull from shallow puddles. Fortunately I never had to pull from mud or livestock ponds; I always found clean looking water.

So what happened? Why was the information so misleading? It turns out Northbounders are traveling through fairly wet seasons when water tables are still high. In fact, every year in the summer, Pennsylvania enters into drought conditions along the Trail, and that New York and New Jersey aren't even all that hydrated to begin with. As far as the section from Virginia to Georgia, well, it just so happens that apart from the dry summer months, 2007 set all sorts of records for drought conditions. By the time I reached Atlanta the media was reporting that they only had 90 days of water left and they were already borrowing from neighbors.

The Watauga Reservoir, Tennessee, in a bad drought.

9. A Walk in Massachusetts

Jugs full of spring water and the canoe that takes you to the spring, at the Upper Goose Pond cabin.

Length:	90 miles	145 km
Max Elevation:	3,491 feet	1,064 m
Min Elevation:	650 feet	198 m
My First Day:	July 27	
My Last Day:	July 31	

What's it like?

Mosquitoes, mud, roots, and NO ski slopes. Massachusetts has a reputation for being one of the two primary "green tunnels" on the AT (the other being Georgia). This derogatory term comes from the many miles you'll be hiking completely enshrouded in trees and vegetation with nary a view to the outside world. Often times the entire AT is broadly characterized as a green tunnel when compared to some of the other long-distance trails in the US. Massachusetts is also therefore quite damp and full of mosquitoes and little pesky black flies.

The state was the height of insect suffering for me, and even though it was too hot for it, I still slept with my sleeping pad. Without it, the black flies could bite me through the hammock fabric AND a silk sleeping bag liner AND a tee-shirt! As it was, I would still be woken up by a nasty bite if a part of my body should leave the safety of the pad.

It's a short state and for the most part the elevation changes that you see involve leaving the mountain ridge to go down in to a populated valley and up the fairly steep slope on the other side. On the plus side, this means you're able to find a grocery store or sandwich shop on or just off the Trail, which means you don't need to carry much food.

Road crossings are very common and this makes it a fairly well hiked state by locals and visitors alike. For better or worse, the ease of access also means that there are a lot of schools and groups using the AT for orientations, team building, etc. This is also where a Southbounder such as me will cross their first major highway, the Mass Turnpike, by way of a fenced-in footbridge.

A few highlights

I'm told that Mount Greylock in the northern part of the state is a really neat place to hike. I'm told that at the top it has a great view, a big monument, buildings and a restaurant. I can tell you that when you have 50 feet of visibility in a cloud bank and pouring rain, the view isn't so great but it really is eerily fascinating to see the monument, pathways and buildings fading in and out of their supernatural fog. As for the restaurant... well... one local warned me that there was construction on the road and that the restaurant had limited hours. Then a sign nailed to a tree a few miles from Greylock, by the operators of Mount Greylock, warned hikers that the restaurant had limited hours. Showing up during those limited hours I then learned that the restaurant was closed for the season entirely.

Freshly picked blueberries for me to carry to the cabin at Upper Goose Pond, so that the cabin caretakers can make blueberry pancakes for all the hikers staying there.

10. Historical Record

Do you have a website?

When I set about planning for the AT, I was excited to be getting away from technology, especially since I'd spent the last seven years engineering software applications. And yet, as much as I wanted to get away, I decided I should build and maintain a website devoted to my experience.

At first the primary purpose was to convey facts about the Trail and answer all the commonly asked questions. It eventually grew into a living creature, complete with an interactive map containing all my checkpoints and a photo gallery with public blog. I wanted to make a site that friends and family could visit on a regular basis to feel like they were part of the journey. It was a huge success. In hindsight I wish I hadn't been so modest about it by keeping it somewhat of a secret amongst people I met on the Trail. I should have had business cards to give out to the folks I met, because so many people wanted to know more about the Trail or simply loved to live vicariously through thru-hikers.

Many people thought I'd have to carry a laptop in order to update my site, not realizing that public internet access is available in most small towns – you just have to look for a library or ask where you find lodging.

I also provided directions to my Base Camp about how to update the site and would often call or text message information to them, normally at least once a week. As for the photo gallery, that was updated only three times while I was on the Trail and two of those times were when I happened to have access to my own computer from home.

Are you going to write a book?

No, I'm not going to write a book. Wait, I mean yes. If you're reading this, then you probably guessed the answer. So, did I always intend to write a book? I always intended to write something even if I wasn't sure on its length or format.

Writing a book about one's AT hike seemed almost cliché, so I spent a lot of time trying to think of ways I could make it unique while still being capable of entertaining and captivating the reader. Many books are simply straight-forward re-tellings of journal entries, and that was certainly not something I wanted to emulate.

Are you going to make a movie?

I didn't carry a video camera and didn't even figure I'd make a slideshow with my photos. And then, while taking a few days off from hiking to attend a hiker conference, I was introduced to multimedia trail movies and knew it was something I wanted to do. I ended up spending weeks identifying photos, cropping them, feeding them in to movie software, choosing transition effects, zooming, inserting music, captions and chapters and in the end I had a 45 minute long "movie" about my hike.

I printed up my own DVD labels and cases and gave away around 60 copies to friends, family and strangers. I loved putting on viewings and doing Q&A sessions before, after or during. My local outfitter even kept a copy for their employees to watch. It proved to be an easy way to share the experience and does a great job showing people how the geography, climate and seasons change.

Do you keep a journal?

At first I bought in to the ultralight hiker lifestyle. My journal was going to be written on whatever paper I had lying around and I would mail those scraps of paper back home so I didn't have to carry them. In the 100 Mile Wilderness I was writing on envelopes, maps, and food packaging. Once I exited the wilderness I felt it would be ludicrous to continue in that fashion, so I bought a cheap drugstore spiral-bound pocket notepad and used that until it was filled up. Then I bought a slightly larger one (for ease of writing) to replace it.

While I didn't write in my journal every day, I did have an entry for every day, often backfilling several at a time if necessary. My entries were generally brief and would consist of things I saw, experienced or thought. Sometimes I would write about who I met or where I stayed.

Apart from daily experiences, the notebook came in handy for keeping track of all my off-trail lodgings and how much each one cost. I used it to take notes whenever someone told me about something I wanted to remember, like "avoid Such-And-Such Hostel, it's filthy" or "you definitely should take that side trail to So-And-So Falls" or even just their name and contact information.

Here are some entries from when I was passing out of Shenandoah National Park in Virginia.

9/11 Rain stopped by morning and turned out to be a good storm. Warned by hikers about a bad hornet nest near Simmons Gap I hike cautiously. It was a huge ground nest! Fortunately I'm upwind of a good breeze so when I step next to the hive they're not expecting me and I instantly break into a sprint! No stings!! I spent a while at Loft Mtn Campstore talking to the keeper and warming up. I also call Gourmet Dave to talk about staying in Waynesboro. Blackrock Mtn had nice views; the shelter a dripping spring and I had it all to myself! Got to hang [my hammock] inside for once!

9/12 It was interesting to leave Shenandoah – the southern end is very empty, humble and feels different. The parkway feels lonely and unused. I like it. Weird to pass all the radio towers, esp the ClearChannel one where a broadcast could be heard inside the little building/shed. Saw a creepy day-hiker and a week-hiker w/70 pound backpacks and a 5 mnth old [Newfoundland dog]! Dave picks me up outside the park and takes me to Krogers and then home. I have a nice night/dinner w/his family.

9/13 Waynseboro… quaint and kinda strange. Seems like it should be friendlier. Postman doesn't accept my Visa because "See ID" isn't a valid signature! What!? Outfitter real nice and well stocked – most alcohol stoves I've seen in one place, Trail angel I called gives me a lift to the trail. OK, now I'm pissed at AT or Wingfoot. I can't find the trail! It's not where it should be and I road walked the Blue Ridge Parkway for 5 miles to Humpback visitor center where I get a BRP map and take a side trail to the AT. Not terrible, and probably a lot shorter, but not my plan. Regardless, I find a primitive cmpgrnd on top of a Mtn w/ a great view! I make a nice fire and settle in. Come morning, as I'm laying in bed, rain starts to fall so I pull everything under the rain fly and pack up. It's a cold rain but doesn't last long. Surprisingly find 2 shelters w/water! Pushing daylight I push for The Priest, a 2,300' climb. It's easy tho, thx to switchbacks, but at the top it's begun to pour rain, it's frigid, and I'm in the clouds w/ low visibility. I do what I can to stay warm and thrilled to find the shelter to myself – I hang inside and settle in to warm/dry clothes. With all the clouds it's a neat time to be on top.

Do you have a camera?

In my mind a camera is something you definitely should find a way to carry. When I was shopping for a camera I was torn between wanting to carry a high quality digital SLR with multiple lenses and a pocket friendly digital lightweight.

I bought two nearly identical cameras from Canon's ultra-compact line - one with a 28mm lens, the other a 32mm - and compared the photos they took in various lighting conditions. I finally decided on the 28mm because it took superior landscape shots and as much as I hoped I'd be taking a lot of close-up wildlife photos, I had a feeling they'd be few and far between.

The camera required proprietary lithium-ion batteries, so I purchased two extras for the trip. I would carry one extra and bounce the other ahead to a location farther down the trail, along with the charger. By rarely needing the flash and relying on only the view-finder (I disabled the little screen) one battery could easily last a month, or about 300 pictures. This meant that I could rotate through my three batteries and only occasionally charge them up.

I did the same thing with memory cards. I hiked with one extra and bounced two ahead to various places on the Trail. You don't want to keep spent cards on you in case they get damaged, but be very careful when mailing them home - I knew several hikers that had their cards lost in the mail and one that had it fall out of an improperly sealed envelope. My AT friend Brit later hiked the Pacific Crest Trail and decided to go to a store to have his photos backed up to a CD where the kiosk physically fried and permanently damaged his card, losing all his photos.

I was fortunate in that I found myself visiting friends, family or home frequently enough that I could personally deliver my cards to safety. Failing that, I'd suggest spending the extra cash to get a cardboard envelope AND have the post office slap some tape over all the seams before mailing it home.

What are your fondest memories?

I ask myself this question and relive the memories often. A lot of them are at the surface, but some bubble up as I see something that triggers a memory. They run the gamut of nature, people and places.

I remember eating freshly made, still warm, granola for breakfast at Elmer's B&B in Hot Springs, North Carolina, and eating and eating and eating. I remember the night before, sitting alone in a six person outdoor hot tub fed by natural hot springs and watching the river roll by.

In stark contrast, I then recall sharing a 15 person hot tub in Maine with three other hikers and a family or two while overlooking a brew pub and tennis courts.

I have oddly fond memories of buying a sub sandwich in Pearisburg, Virginia, and consuming it four hours later at a shelter, surrounded by rhododendrons so dense it felt like night had fallen before the sun had come close to setting.

The industrial size 15 person hot tub just before reaching the Kennebec River in Maine.

Hiking along a bald ridge in North Carolina or Tennessee (hard to know which) with an older couple on their way to their car, laughing with bright smiles on our faces as I held my camera in front of us to take a group photo while we walked in a line. When people see that photo they always ask what we were laughing at and for the life of me I can't recall.

Sunset on my first day in the White Mountains of New Hampshire or sunset from my hammock on the first day in Connecticut or sunset on my second day in the Smoky Mountains.

I certainly didn't sleep well at all but I definitely had a fun time riding out an entire night of 40-50 mph winds in my hammock on a wooded hill top. My rain fly curved against the force of the wind like a sail threatening to blow me away. Four times that night I got out to re-tighten and change the angle of the guy-lines on my rain fly.

The owner of a motel in Tennessee offering me his customary beer and transportation to the local steak house. When I politely told him I don't drink, he expressed how much he appreciated responsible thru-hikers and insisted I take the keys to his mini-van as long as I brought it back by 11pm. I returned it around 9pm.

Texting a friend with my cell phone (not sure why I was texting him or what I was saying) when I looked down and noticed I was stepping over the tail of a Pennsylvania rattlesnake that was gliding off the trail, having seen me long before I saw it. Thirty seconds later my text to him read "Holy cr*p! I almost stepped on a rattler!"

As I was crossing route 17 in New York, I remembered all the times as a kid my family would drive down this highway on our way to Long Island, see the sign for "Appalachian Trail" and wonder what kind of trail it was and who would ever hike it. I hoped that by seeing me as they drove past maybe some kids would be inspired to go hiking or read about the Trail.

Overlooking route 17 in New York.

I found myself salivating one day as I was walking over the crest of a Virginia mountain, only to be greeted by the smell of barbecue. As I hiked, the smell grew stronger, and I figured the only place it could be coming from was a shelter up ahead. Eagerly approaching the shelter, I saw that it was empty, so the smell must be coming from a park near the road just a mile away! The park, the road and the wide river were all lacking the telltale smoke of a barbecue. It turns out that hill, and many more like it over the next few weeks, just happened to be in the peak of wild onion season, and the sun's heat was releasing the most amazing aroma.

I remember at a farm in Massachusetts picking the largest blueberries I'd ever seen and their taste being just as big to match. You'd think you were eating grapes.

Having a geek conversation with a bicyclist at the top of Bear Mountain in New York about his [just released] iPhone and having him use it to take and email me a photo.

I can't say where or when, but I absolutely loved every single time I walked through an evergreen forest drying in the rays of the sun and giving off that clean, crisp, evergreen smell.

The most wonderful and emotional memory is the day after I finished the Trail, sitting in a patio chair at a hotel overlooking the Georgia mountains and calling all my friends and family to tell them I was done!

A photo to remember just how I felt the day after I finished the AT. I sat in the chair for hours, making phone calls and enjoying the view.

11. A Walk in Connecticut

A cascading waterfall pays me a visit while enjoying the flat, packed trail in Connecticut.

Length:	52 miles	84 km
Max Elevation:	2,316 feet	706 m
Min Elevation:	260 feet	79 m
My First Day:	July 31	
My Last Day:	August 3	

What's it like?

When I hit Connecticut, I was elated for one simple reason: it was the first state I could travel through in two or three days! It is one thing to scratch off the miles from your tally sheet, but it's quite another thing entirely to be able to scratch off a whole state from your list.

I like to sum up Connecticut simply by saying "it's a ridge walk followed by a river walk followed by a ridge walk." What I remember most about Connecticut is that I was either on a nice, reasonably flat ridge, or I was on a pedestrian friendly, handicapped accessible (although still dirt and rock) river walk. It was a relaxing state where the shelters seemed to have a good ridge-top view of the valley or were quietly tucked away in a relaxing section of woods.

The Connecticut people do have a reputation for being unfriendly to hikers, but I got along just fine with them and vice versa. Hikers see it as a New York City suburb full of wealth, fancy cars and a fear of vagrants – and if you look like the latter then I imagine you get treated as such. At this point I hadn't shaved in one and a half months but my clothes and equipment looked clean and respectable, so maybe that's why my reception wasn't as frigid as I was lead to believe. Oh, and I did have a reputation for not smelling like a thru-hiker.

A few highlights

I found the river the most enjoyable aspect of the state and, while hiking any of it would be worth the effort, I would probably suggest just hopping on a bicycle and taking the grand tour.

Any section of the AT would probably be nice to do for a day or weekend, especially the places where it passes through a town. It's such a short state that you could easily hike it all over a few weekends.

I tried to find and photograph a four-leaf clover in every state. I only managed to find them in Vermont, Connecticut, Pennsylvania and North Carolina.

A river crossing with no chance of getting your feet wet.

12. Planning

How much does it cost?

Lengthy discussions can arise on the topic of how much a thru-hike costs and in the end the answer usually involves a wide dollar value range. It is commonly said that the AT will require anywhere from $2,500 to $4,500 - or approximately $1 to $2 per mile. Personally, I'm closer to the $4,500 mark and that includes gear I had to purchase before and during the hike, lodging, food/supplies, and transportation to/from the trail.

If I'd known ahead of time exactly what weather I'd hit, I could have probably saved $500 on gear, but I lost my crystal ball to a gang of fortune tellers who had fallen on bad times. If I was willing to let my diet suffer I could easily save another $500 - but that was not a risk worth taking.

One of the biggest money savers is to simply hit a town for supplies and keep on moving, rather than succumb to the Siren call of fresh linens and eating for hours on end in front of a TV. There are plenty of places where you can get a shower or do laundry without having to pay for a room or spend the night. Personally, I fully bought in to the idea that motels were morale boosters and are thus acceptable alternatives to roughing it in the woods.

Some people hope to save money by preparing food supplies before they leave for the Trail and using mail drops instead of grocery stores. Certainly a three day resupply from a convenience store can be quite costly but, then again, shipping a box of food from home isn't exactly free. Of the people I knew who prepared ahead of time, most were unsure if it actually saved money but all felt that at least it wasn't more expensive. Perhaps more importantly, they felt like their diets were healthier. I must admit that buying several days worth of food from a 7-Eleven does make me question my sanity.

If you haven't camped much before, it can certainly be a costly venture. Maybe the gear you started with was inadequate and you had to replace your stove, sleeping bag or shelter. One fellow started in Maine with five (yes five!) pocket knives when even one is considered optional, a full cook set (large and small pots, kettle, two frying pans) when one small pot would suffice, and two stoves in case one failed. He could have saved a lot of money, if he'd just done a little research.

And research is certainly advised! Visit your local outfitter, hear what they have to say and make a list of what they tried to sell you. When you get home, do some asking around and internet searching to find out if you really do need a candle lantern with carrying case and stand, or if that expensive backpack is any better than that cheap one.

Did you break in your shoes ahead of time?

I'd recommend, of course, that you break in the first pair of shoes. It's not only important that you wear them around town and on hikes, but I learned there's a huge difference between 10 pounds on your back over one day and 30 pounds over two days.

Over time your arches will flatten and your feet will change shape as you carry more weight. If the toe area (or toe box) of your shoes isn't just right, you may lose your toe nails from the constant pounding and rubbing – perhaps without even knowing it.

So that first pair is a no-brainer, but what about the others? Should you buy several pairs ahead of time and break them all in? Should you find someone back home with the same shoes size to wear the next pair?

It's hard to say just how much your feet will change once you get going, so I don't recommend buying any shoes ahead of time. There will be plenty of places on the Trail to buy new ones and even numerous hostels with old shoe bins where sometimes you can find a practically brand new pair cast aside by a hiker that didn't find them comfortable.

In hindsight, I should have more rigorously tested my footwear ahead of time. The day and weekend hikes I went on were no comparison to the abuse caused by carrying all that weight day after day, especially in mud and rain. And it's not only about shoes but also the insoles you choose to use with them – be it the ones that came with them or the aftermarket variety.

How did you arrange transport to/from?

Northbounders and Southbounders need to figure out how exactly they intend to get to the start of the Trail. Southbounders will generally want to start, and stay the night, in Baxter State Park. This will require reservations made in advance. If you can't make a reservation, the alternatives are to hike Katahdin and plan on enough time left in the day to hike out of the park; or start outside the park and hike in to the free (to people hiking in on the AT) campground.

That's it. Once you're there, you simply go with the flow and make your choices as they come.

In my case, I was lucky that my friend, Adam, and his father were willing to drive me to Baxter. If Adam's not available for your hike, there is always the Trail Angel and shuttle network throughout Maine and Georgia willing to provide hikers with transport. The internet can help you find them. Many times local lodgings will have their own shuttle or know where to find one.

You can fly to the nearest airport, take a bus to the closest Trail town, stay at a motel and in the morning catch a ride with the owner to the start of the AT. You'll need to research the options that best suit you.

These same shuttles and Angels can be used to leave the Trail too. Before you finish your journey, you can email or phone them to establish a pickup date and time. You can do this as far in advance as you wish, but realize that if you start calling around a day before you finish, you might have to dial with your fingers crossed. When I finished, I could have had someone pick me up and drive me directly to the Atlanta airport if I wanted... although in my case I had a friend pick me up to spend some time playing tourist, before hopping a bus to Florida for some beach time.

If you're leaving the Trail unexpectedly, there are always bus routes, hitchhiking, friendly locals, airports, etc., up and down the Trail. Chances are if you come in to a hostel or motel with an injury or illness, the proprietor will take pity on you and drive you to the bus station or airport.

Did you train ahead of time?

On the one hand I don't think proper training can hurt, on the other hand I wouldn't say it's necessary. I'm a big fan of letting the body adapt to its surroundings and that includes the sometimes arduous effort of going from sedentary cubicle worker to trail churning outdoor enthusiast. It might take time, but assuming you're not otherwise hindered by pre-existing genetic or medical conditions, preventing your body from this metamorphosis, just about anyone should be able to thru-hike without undertaking an exercise regimen beforehand.

I didn't do anything beyond my normal routine, which coincidentally included a 40-mile round-trip bicycle commute for work several days a week with weekends full of hiking, boating, cutting and hauling wood, etc. I'm certain that these activities helped me to start with high mileage days on the AT, but there's nothing that says you can't start off slow.

I'm no Doctor or professor of sports medicine, but there are certain aspects to training for a long hike that seem logical to me. The basis for my reasoning comes from an examination of how my body changed over the course of 2,200 miles.

First, I don't see any reason to bulk up your upper body unless you're carrying a duffle bag instead of a backpack. You don't need a lot of muscle up there and if you're a toothpick to begin with you'll soon have all the muscle you need - which won't be a lot.

Second, while I think bicycle training is beneficial for everyone (hiker or not), I wouldn't get caught up in it too much for the Trail. My legs were built mostly of bicycle muscle and I figured this would give me an advantage, but judging by life after the AT, I can clearly see that I lost a good portion of that and it was replaced by walking muscles. Clearly the two were not made equal, and my body adjusted. This isn't to say that 100% of bicycle muscle is useless for hiking, far from it, but that the benefits of biking is more in how it helps your cardiovascular system.

The key areas that I feel are important and worth focusing on are cardiovascular and knee/ankle strengthening workouts. Biking and running certainly help with both of these aspects, and will definitely help your hike. I believe that the efficiency with which your body processes energy and waste are bigger factors than how bulked up you are, and a regimen of cardiovascular activities will aid this process.

While your upper body will, relatively speaking, be on vacation for several months, your lower body will not only have to carry you day after day, but it will be supporting the weight of your backpack as well. Knee injuries are common, as are stress fractures, and I'd encourage everyone to take some preventative measures. Talk to a physical therapist or sports physician about some recommended exercises. Having just had knee surgery, and having seen a physical therapist a few years prior about weak ankles, I was already aware of my options and limits.

Oh... I'm too old...

Wait one second while I drop the needle on this broken record. There are a lot of people out there who apparently have always wanted to do the AT but when life finally gave them time for it, they felt they were too old. OK, yes, true, there are many legitimate age related factors that should be taken into account - I met several individuals who suffered broken bones in their feet/ankle while simply taking a bad step on a flat, smooth sidewalk. The problem was ultimately that of naturally brittle bones after 1,500 miles of poor nutrition - or so they claimed.

I'm not really all that interested in addressing the numerous age related complaints, but rather want to point out that most of the time these are hogwash. After the college graduate demographic, retired folks are the second largest percentage of thru-hikers and are seemingly just as likely to complete the entire length as anyone else.

The bottom line is that any age can hike from end to end; you just have to understand your limits. If you need to go a little slower, so be it, or maybe you should take more time off when you hit town. I can't urge you enough to eat well and listen to your body. Consider taking dietary supplements and learn to carry as little in your pack as possible so that you can maybe carry a little extra food instead. My guess is that if you're already making excuses for why you can't do it, then you're probably already doomed to failure anyway, and that's a shame.

Oh... I'm too out of shape...

This is really just more of the same. Unlike age, however, this one is a little more cut and dried. People of all body types hike the Trail with success. Obese, non-athletic or even skinny-to-the-point-of-fragile people successfully complete thru-hikes. I passed a guy around his 1,500th mile who was around 5' 10", weighing an estimated 100 pounds. In an unhealthy way, he seemed to have absolutely no muscle or fat anywhere on his body. I commented to another Northbounder later in the day that I was worried about the kid. I was told that he actually started in Georgia looking like that and he's been just fine. Apparently it's just his natural physique.

Many people quit in the first few weeks because they can't handle the stress of carrying all that weight or putting one tired leg in front of the other. It seems, however, that for almost everyone around the four to six week time frame their body will adapt to the physical demands and cease to be a concern - for some it can be as little as two weeks. While there is certainly a fair amount of muscle required for this to happen, literature will tell you that it's also important for the body to learn how to pump out the lactic acid as well as quickly digest food into energy. The shame of it is that so many people give up before ever reaching this milestone because they mentally can't endure the first few weeks.

Of course I'm speaking in generalities, and I'm sure there are some people who are too out of shape or incapable of adjusting to life on the Trail. But you never know until you try! I know people that were 100 pounds overweight when they started their successful thru-hike.

13. A Walk in New York

Just after passing through the Bear Mountain Zoo, and just before heading up the mountain, is this family-friendly recreational lake.

Length:	88 miles	142 km
Max Elevation:	1,433 feet	437 m
Min Elevation:	124 feet	38 m
My First Day:	August 3	
My Last Day:	August 9	

What's it like?

I like New York because, after traveling nearly directly in a north/south line through Vermont, Massachusetts and Connecticut, you suddenly hit the New York border and find yourself taking a course correction. You are heading southwest, directly to New Jersey. It's what I call a "transi-

Transitioning from Connecticut to New York.

tion state," where you are moving from one part of the AT to another. In this case you are leaving New England behind while at the same time changing direction and simultaneously moving from one ridge of the Appalachians to another. You have left the mosquitoes and black flies behind, and you have hit the tail end of the northbound thru-hikers. In New York and New Jersey, I was inundated with wild blueberries and blackberries growing along the Trail, but sadly it was the last time I would have such a treat.

While Connecticut was the last place where I had problems with black flies biting me, New York was where I began to encounter the non-biting, annoying kind of fly that loves to just buzz your ear and try to get into your eyes. To one degree or another I had to deal with these little guys until Georgia. Fortunately, I could keep them away from my face and ears just by carrying a branch (with or without leaves) and occasionally waving it around my head. If they got to be really bad, or I felt like giving my arms a rest, I would tuck leaves up under my bandana or hat to cover my ears or forehead. Both methods were extremely useful. I really, REALLY, don't like bugs buzzing my ears and face!

I was not expecting the drastic terrain differences and I loved it. In one day I would find myself walking through cow pastures, then rocky, exposed ridges followed by dense forest. The trail itself could be hard and littered with loose rocks or packed earth.

The AT passes within 40 miles of New York City and that alone makes for an interesting experience. You will find yourself crossing several major highways, going through a modest zoo, crossing the Hudson River on a toll bridge, deciding whether or not to stay at a monastery (on their baseball field), and crisscrossing a spiraling roadway as you race against cars to the top of Bear Mountain. Just like in New Jersey, you will find a creamery or two, one of which is just a few hundred feet from the AT.

A few highlights

It's probably not as interesting for a weekend hiker, but near Pawling, New York the AT crosses an active passenger train line. Where it crosses there is a nice bench with a sign declaring it to be an actual stop for the Appalachian Trail. On weekends you can travel between this stop and Grand Central Station in NYC.

The Bear Mountain and Harriman State Park regions of the AT would make for nice hikes. Bear Mountain may have hordes of tourists on a nice weekend, especially during the fall, but the view is spectacular. The eastern side of the mountain is more populated and might cause you to wonder why you didn't just drive to the top, but once you begin descending down the western slope you can feel the civilization slipping away and the quiet of the woods returning.

Bear Mountain sits inside Harriman State Park and as you head west from the summit you go deeper into the park. The woods, lakes and ponds here are a real treat, especially in the heat of summer. I would only caution that bear sightings

The tower atop Bear Mountain. A parking lot is on the other side.

are common here due to a history of negligent hikers who have trained them to come looking for free food.

A tunnel through the foliage with wooden planks to keep hikers from eroding the soil

14. Hiking (Curiosity)

How do you know where you're going?

For most people, the hardest part is getting to the Trail in the first place. Once you're there it's very easy to follow as long as you remember which direction you're heading – which is apparently harder than you'd think.

The AT makes use of white paint splotches, or "blazes," about the size and shape of a $1 bill (or any US bill if you'd prefer) placed at mostly random distances on trees, rocks, road signs, bridges or street lampposts. Sometimes you may have to look down on the ground to find it or turn around to see it on the backside of something. These are very distinctive and generally are not used for any other official trail system markings in the area so as to avoid confusion. If you're anywhere near the AT and you see a white blaze on a tree, I'd wager you're on the AT.

Side trails that connect to the AT are blazed with blue of roughly the same dimensions. If you're unsure where you are and you come upon a blue blaze anywhere near the AT, you pretty much have a 50% chance that one direction will take you to the AT - the other direction could go to a parking lot, road, campground, scenic overlook, water source, another trail and so on.

It's not uncommon for someone to wake up in the morning, pack up camp and start hiking the wrong direction. Or stop for lunch and forget which direction they came from. In these cases it doesn't take long until they pass a familiar landmark or see a sign that tells them what then seems blatantly obvious.

Folks that are particularly forgetful when it comes to these sorts of things are instructed to pitch their tent, or lay their sleeping bag, in a certain direction that will remind them. "Ah, my door opens up THAT way, so THAT way must be where I am heading today."

I was never disoriented like that and for the most part there will be a "North / South" sign on or near many shelters to remind you.

I did, however, find the snowmobile/ATV trails in Maine to be particularly annoying. They will run with the AT for a while, leave, come back, crisscross and forever leave it. Numerous times I'd hike half a mile without a white blaze and wonder if I'd accidentally followed an ATV trail. In one day I did leave the trail twice only to realize it half a mile too late.

In Tennessee and North Carolina, the fallen leaves would completely cover the tops of wide, rocky, forested ridges, making it impossible to see the impression of the trail. For some reason, on one particular ridge the blazes were considerably far apart and often I'd wonder if I was even heading in the right direction. Usually in these cases, just as you start to look around and wonder when the last time was you saw a blaze, one will suddenly appear in the distance.

At nearly every road crossing is a reminder that Southbounders are a minority. You will exit the woods, hit the road, and look around, having no idea where the trail enters the woods on the other side. You turn around and right where you left the woods you see a nice, big sign that says "AT North" along with a nice white blaze. Turning back around you look hard for something similar in your direction... but there's nothing. At this point the easiest thing to do is look at the northbound white blaze and based on where it's painted you can infer the direction the Northbounder would be walking in order to see it. "In order to see that blaze a Northbounder would have to be walking in THIS direction, so if I go in THAT direction... Ah ha! There's an opening in the woods, but I don't see a blaze or a sign..." and then 20 feet into the woods you'll finally see a blaze.

Okay, OK, I'm being a bit cranky, not ALL road crossings are like that but I can assure you there were plenty. Northbounders do have better signage all along the Trail.

My favorite road crossing had, on the northbound side of the road, a big arrow with an "N" and a caricature of TWO hikers walking together. On the other side of the road, in my direction, there was an arrow with an "S" and a caricature of ONE lonely hiker. I have a feeling this was not coincidence but rather someone with a subtle sense of humor.

Signs on opposite sides of the road. Clearly someone maintaining this section has a sense of humor. I'm such a lonely Southbounder. At least I don't have a doppleganger mirroring my movements!

There was one time in particular when I didn't exactly get lost, but I didn't exactly know where the Trail was. When you leave the Shenandoah National Park in Virginia, you follow the park road across a highway and immediately after begins the Blue Ridge Parkway. Somewhere around that road crossing, the AT heads back into the woods. I missed it. I walked a mile down the road and thought it strange that they didn't provide any blazes for southbound OR northbound hikers. I turned around and walked a mile back to where I last saw a blaze. I then walked VERY slowly south and looked everywhere for a blaze or even something that looked like a trail. I didn't see it so I decided that it had to be the road.

After a few miles of road walking I figured that I really, truly, was not on the AT. My AT handbook suggested that after about four or five miles the AT would cross the Parkway, so I figured I'd just keep walking and eventually I'd see the Trail. And so it was that after about four miles I hit a visitor center where I could fill up my water bottles, use the restroom and look at a map to see that the AT was basically across the road and down a short side trail.

Almost a year later I drove that stretch of Parkway to see if I could find the seemingly invisible trailhead. I found it, but it wasn't easy. I've driven by a few times with passengers in the car, creeping slowly past the trailhead, and challenged them to find where the AT enters the woods. They can't.

Small guide books can be purchased that enumerate every spring, stream, river, pond, mountain summit, road crossing, fire road, shelter, camp ground, landmark and town. Pretty much every thru-hiker will carry a guide and/or a set of maps. The maps aren't as detailed as the guides about the Trail itself, but they do provide better information about the region around the AT corridor.

Do you ever build a fire?

A camp fire on the AT is an issue worth talking about. If everyone were to have a fire, the dead wood would disappear and people would start to kill living trees. Generally, fires are discouraged unless it's an emergency. It's not illegal (unless there's a park regulation or drought condition to make it so) but it's frowned upon from an environmental impact point of view. I ran in to inexperienced people all the time that believe cutting a living tree is a perfectly acceptable method of gathering firewood – unaware that dry dead-fall burns much easier and better anyway.

That said, it all depends. In Maine, there was so much dead fall that it seemed better to burn it in a controlled manner than leave it to accumulate. One couple was using it as their only means of cooking - and they cooked three meals a day! I can't begin to imagine how long their thru-hike took.

One section-hiker I met was from Germany and fully bought in to what he called the "John Wayne way of life." He insisted on having tremendous bonfires that would last all night and still be burning by morning. That is, he used to build bonfires, until I convinced him that in those cowboy movies the fires were still burning in the morning not because they built huge fires but because someone would wake up and add more wood throughout the night.

If you're going to have a fire, it's generally best to keep it as small and utilitarian as possible. I was glad the German bonfire artist understood and obeyed the safety aspects, but he didn't understand the environmental impacts. The light pollution alone is enough to bother some hikers, then there's the waste of it and the scar it leaves on the land.

I helped build plenty of fires that were used by groups of people, but only twice did I build a fire for just myself. I hiked in a light rain that stopped just before reaching an empty campground. The woods were dark and had a very eerie feeling to them. I put on my headlamp and made my way around camp looking for wood and built a fire so that I could dry out and feel more comfortable in my surroundings.

The other time I made a fire was down near the Blue Ridge Parkway of Virginia when I found myself all alone on top of a mountain at a primitive camp site. Across the wide valley, on another mountain top much like my own, I could see the lights of what could have been a house or a building for the parkway. It was such a nice, clear night and I decided to watch the twinkling lights around the valley while warming to a fire.

Do you ever build a fire? (part 2)

Well... I did attempt to build a fire one other time just for me. On top of a wooded hill, sandwiched between farm lands, I made camp by myself. It was a calm, cool night and I was deep in sleep when a noise startled me awake. I sat up and listened. I heard it again, something large rustling the leaves in the exact direction and distance of my food bag.

Whatever it was stayed in that area for a while and logic told me it must be a bear trying to get my hanging food. I called out and shuffled the fabric of my hammock but the intruder didn't even hesitate. I grew worried, thinking that this bear was not afraid of me, and worse, now it might approach my hammock out of curiosity!

As the minutes passed, I grew protective of my food and decided I should do something if I wanted to see my dried pineapple again. The Velcro on the hammock as I exited was loud but that didn't even scare it. I dropped in to my shoes and squatted with my headlamp on, trying to see this "edibles thief" - but my headlamp doesn't throw its light very far.

I picked up whatever sticks I could find nearby and started shouting while banging them together. Nothing. Now I knew I was in trouble, this bear wasn't spooked by anything. And then the rustling changed and began heading in my direction!

I panicked and looked for options. In seconds I cleared a circle in the forest floor of debris and dropped in a pile of twigs. I grabbed hold of some spare pieces of paper (news articles sent by my friend) and lit one, hoping that a fire would scare it off. I was trying to build a fire too quickly and in my haste I was failing. As the noise got closer, I decided to just light the whole piece of paper and start waving it while dancing about.

Finally, with my dinky little headlamp and my sheet of flaming paper I was able to illuminate the scene and see that this giant beast of a bear was in fact an adolescent deer now about 15 feet away from me and stopped in its tracks. In my mind I heard Adam say "Stupid squirrels."

Relieved, I came to realize as the night wore on that I had camped in a popular deer feeding ground. That deer, even the five others that joined him, didn't care at all about my food bag, I just happened to hang it over their flora grocery store. I didn't sleep much that night - they kept waking me up and I kept trying to scare them off so I could sleep. Occasionally I would grab my camera, reach my hand out of my hammock, and blindly take a few flash photos of the dark woods. I could then count the number of glowing eyes to see how many deer had come for the feast.

What about shaving?

The stereotypical dirty thru-hiker I was not. I did experiment with a beard for the first month, but I didn't like it and I'll never do it again!

The photos will show that from Maine to New Jersey I did not shave. I grew a manly thicket of scruff that looked unkempt while simultaneously earning me respect from fellow hikers - "Ah, he has to be a thru-hiker, look at that beard!"

Around Connecticut, however, I started to feel dirty, hot and realized that to non-hikers the beard said "don't trust him." I had the option of trimming it to look intentional (rather than the lazy look) or to shave it off entirely. When I hit New Jersey, I bought a dozen disposable razors and used three of them to remove the unwelcome follicles from my face -

leaving the other razors behind for fellow hikers who may be tempted to do the same.

About once every two or three weeks thereafter, I'd take the time to shave. I felt lighter, healthier, cleaner and less like a vagrant. My clean face, combined with my relatively clean-looking clothes, meant that thru-hikers would mistake me for a casual hiker and feel no need to stop me to talk. Although a tad insulting, it also meant fewer interruptions. I also found that people in town were more accepting of me and business operators more accommodating.

Nicest section? Hardest?

Which of your children is your favorite? It's hard to say which sections were the nicest and hardest. I liked different sections differently and the same can be said for difficulty. But certain images do keep coming to mind when I hear the phrase "nicest section."

Maine was a great state overall because of the varied terrain and the wonderfully isolated mountain views. Its 100 Mile Wilderness provided very fond memories of bogs and fording rivers (something you won't find elsewhere on the AT).

I'm a sucker for river walks and so Connecticut has a special place in my heart as the Trail was gorgeously placed alongside the Housatonic River.

Skip ahead to central and southern Virginia along the Blue Ridge Parkway where mountain ranges, sculpted by water erosion, resemble well-manicured fingers holding down the valleys and plains.

And in Tennessee and North Carolina, I found myself once again among charismatic river valleys dug deep into the landscape.

I wouldn't say that any part of the Trail is technically difficult - you won't need climbing gear or safety harnesses, if that's what you're thinking. But, yes, there are plenty of times when you'll be on all fours scrambling around, trying to avoid a wicked slide. The steep ups and downs will require a lot of knee strength or patience. Of particular note here are the Whites and Presidential Range in New Hampshire (covered elsewhere in this book). Many would say that Pennsylvania not only kills shoes but puts a permanent stumble in your stride - I personally found the mud and tree root filled trails of Vermont and Massachusetts to be more of a nuisance.

You might also hear complaints about the boredom of Georgia's or Massachusetts' "green tunnel," which taxes your mental fortitude by depriving your senses of stimulation. Some find it hard to walk for mile upon mile surrounded by dense greenery with no significant views.

The trail in Tennessee and North Carolina was taxing on the mind as you find yourself going up, up, up, up only to learn there's no view and the only way you know you've reached the top is because you start going down, down, down.

But at least there were switchbacks in Tennessee and North Carolina. In Maine, the trail just goes straight up to the top and back down the other side. In many places, some very patient trail crews put in stones steps just to make your knees burn even more.

I have fond memories of rare gems, like a once-developed ridge top where rectangular plots of land once held houses, but are now grassy fields pushing back the encroaching forest - the old road has become a footpath. I remember a shelter placed just a short throw from a gorgeous stream; a rocky vista affording endless views; the top of an isolated fire tower looking down at a vast expanse of fall foliage; Maryland with its oddly placed monuments to battles and people of old.

It seems predictable to say McAfee Knob and the nearby Tinker Cliffs were visual highlights with their sweeping views of the Virginia landscape.

One place I desperately want to get back to is the Grayson Highlands in southern Virginia, where the wild ponies of Assateague and Chincoteague fame originate and run free. The land is remote, rocky, barren, covered in fields of grass and wildflowers and feels out of place on the East coast.

The Whites

Perspective definitely plays with your head here, and when it comes to the Whites there are two rules you have to follow: 1. don't trust everything you hear, 2. the Whites are what you want them to be.

It's safe to say that the White Mountains of New Hampshire are the most rugged and daunting section of the Trail, while simultaneously the most breathtaking. Northbounders have been hearing stories about this part of the AT for 1,700 miles and the large majority of them are anxious to see just how demanding it is. Southbounders have been going through some relatively hard terrain since we started, so we're anxious to get through them and on to the "flat and easy" trail beyond.

The Presidential Mountains contained in the Whites are home to Mount Washington, a peak famous for recording the northern hemisphere's highest wind speed (at 231 mph the gauge broke) and habitually known to dump snow on hikers and tourists in any month. There are two significant stretches where you are entirely above tree line without any break from the wind or weather - the longest at 12.7 miles includes Mount Washington, the other is around six miles in length. In bad weather, these areas can be daunting or deadly. On July 1, 2007, just four days before I entered the Whites, an inch of snow fell on Mount Washington. The day I went up and over the "big W" it was 40°F (4.5°C) with 40 mph winds and I was inside a cloud bank the entire day with rain whipping sideways and 50 feet of visibility. Several times I was fortunate enough to be standing next to a tall rock cairn when the wind managed to knock me over and I didn't have far to fall.

Lodging establishments called Huts are scattered throughout the Whites. In essence, the Huts are medium and large log cabin structures where, in return for around $100, you are provided with a bed, blanket, pillow, running water, limited electricity, dinner, breakfast and brief entertainment. Power is provided by solar and gas generators, the water comes from springs/wells and all the food is backpacked in by the staff and cooked on gas stoves. As an alternative, there are far cheaper pay-for-stay campgrounds providing a tent platform, outhouse and a large metal box to keep food away from animals. Even fewer are some non-staffed, free, primitive campgrounds. At a Hut, generally speaking, thru-hikers can partake in what is called work-for-stay where you help out by doing dishes, sweeping, cleaning, etc., and in return you get a warm place to stay and two hearty meals for free. Thru-hikers can even earn their keep by talking to the tourists or being recruited as entertainment in the form of song and dance routines.

The major issue with these megalith mountains is the mythology itself. Nowhere else on the Trail was there so much misinformation and I wracked my brain trying to figure out why. Before I entered the Whites, 100% of the Northbounders I talked to (about 15) specifically about the Whites said basically the same thing: the ups and downs were killer; there's either NO work-for-stay or it's really hard to get it; and most of the Hut staff are jerks. They go on to say that if you can't afford the Huts or the $8 for a campground, your only alternative is to go "stealth" and pitch your tent where you hopefully won't be caught. Every week the trail maintainers identify stealth camping spots and cover them with debris and/or large rocks.

This is what "they" say, not what I say.

A view of Franconia Ridge while sheltered just below the summit of Mount Moosilauke, my last day in the Whites.

And so, us Southbounders were afraid of the Whites and were always looking for advice on where these stealth spots were so we could cheaply make it through - there were even stories about hikers that would walk six hours, nap for two, and repeat ad infinitum for several days, thereby never needing a place to stay for the night.

Lies, lies and more lies. The Whites, for me and the dozen Southbounders I spoke with, was a friendly place where work-for-stay was easy to find and the staff were all eager to shelter and talk to us - even though this was the height of thru-hiker season. The ups and downs were long and tedious but hardly worthy of the boundless tales.

As for camping, it turns out you can pitch your tent anywhere you please, as long as it's not within a quarter mile of a Hut or fee campground. This means you can camp almost anywhere for free. Not only that, the AT crosses in and out of national forest and state park lands, and in the national forest there are free, un-supervised, primitive campgrounds. Each one has convenient wooden tent platforms (or in my case hammock patios).

However, due to the distance between national forest campgrounds, it's unlikely that you could subsist solely on them for your trip through the Whites.

Official policy states that no more than two hikers can be part of work-for-stay, but unofficially there is no policy. I stayed at three Huts and one of them had nine hikers taking part in work-for-stay. The only down side

An example of a "Hut"; this one at Lake of the Clouds, just below the summit of Mount Washington.

then is that there might not be a lot of Hut food to go around, which is a small price to pay for running water, warmth and dry shelter.

At one Hut I asked what the guidelines were for the work-for-stay program and it all came down to a few simple rules. In the case of bad weather you will always have a roof over your head, but you might not get fed, depending on when you show up and who was there before you. If the weather is fair and you show up asking for work-for-stay before 2pm, chances are you will be told to keep hiking in order to be fair to those who show up exhausted towards the end of the day - that's considered just plain lazy.

Circumstances play into it all the time - I showed up a little after 2pm to a less popular Hut just for some warm soup, shelter from the rain, and a chance to warm up before pushing on. The fellow in charge begged me to stay, claiming the weather wasn't good for the stretch ahead and that he wanted to hear my stories. My arm was twisted and as the hours went by, two more thru-hikers arrived for the night. Normally we would find a spot of floor in the dining room, a table top or even a bench to slumber away the night, but that night there were so many tourist cancellations that one of the three bunk houses was completely empty. We were urged to each choose a room, spread out our gear to dry and enjoy a quiet bunk. Amazing hospitality.

So then why is there so much misinformation coming out of this part of the Trail? I find it hard to believe that people are blatantly lying, and I find it hard to believe that things are really that bad. When I got through the Whites, I met many Northbounders asking if the horror stories were true. Inquiring about the source of this nonsense I was told that it came directly from my fellow Southbounders. However, after the Whites, I caught up with or emailed the 12 Sobo's in front of me and all of them said they had a great time in the Whites.

In the end, I think it simply comes down to "garbage in, garbage out." If you enter the Whites expecting each Hut to be run by a bunch of drugged-up jerks in charge of hundred-dollar-a-night tourist traps, that's what you'll find. If you feel like, as a thru-hiker, you deserve a discount or special treatment, think again. From my research ahead of time I was indeed predisposed to have a negative view of the Hut system, but I refused to let it affect my behavior once I was there. I did witness a lot of hiker ego and I know some of them were habitually rude to the Hut staff just on principle. I loved the Huts and their staff!

Where do you sleep?

It seems that at least half of Northbounders slept solely in shelters and opted to leave their tents at home. Shelters are reasonably spaced along the length of the whole Trail. Overcrowding, garbage, animals, or even collapsed roofs (from fallen trees) can make them uninhabitable, so you're taking a small gamble by relying on them. Commonly refered to as lean-tos, these three-walled structures are a tradition in the Adirondack Mountains and range from old and decrepit to new and multi-storied with balconies. On only five nights did I sleep on the wooden floor of a shelter - it was a failed experiment to see if I'd prefer it. A few hikers even "cowboy camp," which means they sleep on the ground without even a tent, but I don't know any who used that as their primary means.

I opted for my Hennessy Hammock with custom rain fly (my Black-Eyed Susie, named after the Blackbishop design and Susie, my wonderful seamstress friend who helped me construct it). The hammock is amazingly comfortable (almost to its detriment!) and yet it isn't necessarily lighter than some of the tents in the ultralight market. My model has a built-in mosquito net and accessory line for conveniently hanging small items inside.

For maybe three of the four and a half months, I almost always hung my hammock near a shelter or campground. I did this because it usually meant a water supply and privy (separate but equal amenities!) nearby. In

My rain fly strung up between two trees with the reflective guy-lines staked to the ground. My hammock is barely visible up against the ridgeline of the rain fly. That's my gear on the ground.

the last month and a half, with the drought in full effect, there was rarely a water supply, so it was commonplace for me to simply camp wherever I was when the sun went down - even more so when in the privy-less state of Tennessee.

While tent campers had to find flat, level ground, I simply needed two trees 15-30 feet apart. Sounds easy, but with the proliferation of bushy rhododendrons in the south or even the numerous and barren cow pastures, it sometimes took some effort. This was hardly a significant problem but there is one related downside to hammocks: you can't hang them on a bald or exposed summit. Many times I was jealous of the hikers who could pitch their tent in a gorgeous meadow and enjoy a sunrise or sunset. While I could have probably cowboy camped, I'd much rather sleep comfortably in my hammock.

I'd often "hang" on steep slopes, which was awfully convenient while at the same time comically awkward since shoes, water bottles and sleeping bags love to roll downhill. Not to mention the difficulty of waking up for a late night bathroom break, clumsily stumbling out of the hammock, and trying to stay upright while my legs and feet wanted to go sliding out from under me.

Once the crowds died down, somewhere around the half-way point, I found myself alone at more and more shelters. On these occasions, I would hang my hammock under the protective roof, often with half of my 12 foot hammock under the main structure and the other half under the porch roof. Doing so, I was able to avoid bad weather or even just biting cold winds.

Because it is considered rude to "hang" in a shelter while someone sleeps on the floor, I only allowed myself to do that once. On that occasion, I arrived well after

I manage to find a Vermont shelter all to myself but I still hang my hammock.

sunset in the pouring rain with winds so strong trees were snapping all over the place. Fortunately the shelter was so big that I wasn't at all in the way and I had strong approval from the other occupants. Ultimately, the hammock bug netting that night acted like a dew collector as it trapped all the moisture in the passing cloud bank and deposited it inside with me - so I ended up sleeping on the floor of the lean-to after all. If you can call it sleep... more than once I left the shelter to see just how big a branch or tree had landed on the metal roof.

There is quite a lot of luxury to be found on the Appalachian Trail actually. From yuppie shelters with multiple floors, running water/showers, and pizza delivery; to private cabins converted to hiker havens. For example, the 501 Shelter in Pennsylvania is a large, fully enclosed square building with a domed skylight, dozens of bunks, solar shower, two doors and functional glass windows - there's also a ranger station next door. Eckville Shelter, also in Pennsylvania, sits next to a caretaker house (donated to the AT) and features a solar shower, running water and library with board games. The shelter at Fontana Dam, North Carolina, is nicknamed the "Fontana Hilton" because of the beautiful construction, hot showers and running water.

Many shelters have fire places inside the building or even a fourth wall, some even have regular or sliding doors. On the Tennessee and North Carolina border sits the very popular Overmountain Shelter. The shelter is an old, red, two story barn at the edge of a large farm. The bottom floor is an old livestock area with one side open to the elements. The top floor can comfortably house dozens of campers.

Hikers who choose to leave behind their tent or hammock in favor of shelters will usually save weight as well as the time required each day to set up or break camp. However, they will have to deal with one of the most unpleasant aspects of the trail: snoring. My rule of thumb is that as long as there's even one person in the shelter there will be snoring - even if you are that one person. Please, if you snore, especially if you snore badly, do us all a favor and sleep somewhere else. In a gorgeous two story cabin (Upper Goose Pond in Massachusetts) 15 weary hikers were kept awake all night by the worst snorer I had ever heard. It was so bad that, rather than take advantage of a real mattress upstairs, a few of us opted to sleep on the hard wood floor downstairs without sleeping pads. Setting the right example, that same night one guy actually slept outside on the mosquito filled porch because he claimed he was a bad snorer - follow his example!

Do you ever stay in town?

I'm not sure if I would be considered a "townie" (someone addicted to towns) but I definitely took advantage of civilization. In the beginning I felt that towns were a way to get a good night's sleep and gorge myself on calories. Some people felt that staying the night in town was somehow cheating, that you were no longer roughing it. Inhabiting the back of my mind was this thought, but I soon realized that the motels and hostels are a huge part of the Trail's life and history. Two of the most famous thru-hikers, Earl Shaffer and Gramma Gates, made towns a part of their story since the AT used to run smack dab through the middle of many towns and villages. Businesses are as much a part of the Trail as the hikers.

At least I would try to stay at what I'd consider the most historically important accommodations rather than just the cheapest - often the two went hand in hand though. And, yes, there were times when I simply felt the need for a shower, television and a bed that didn't require two trees to set up - but mostly I looked forward to a night in town so that I could buy lots of food and lie in bed, eating to my heart's content. My favorite in-bed meal was microwaved nacho cheese dip, tortilla chips, beets, Kefir yogurt drink, fruit salad, mixed salad, and banana pudding while watching a Dirty Jobs marathon on television.

Early in the trip I realized that I never slept well in bunk rooms, which was how most hostels were built. Before I'd even left Maine I had decided that it was better to spend the money on a private room just so I could better restore my constitution.

Even with a room to myself, I found I wasn't sleeping well and I chalked it up to me being used to my comfy hammock. But, once I noticed a pattern forming, I was finally able to enjoy my overnights in town. You see, before the Trail, I could drink a liter of Mountain Dew before bed and still sleep soundly. No matter what I drank or ate I could always fall asleep quickly and deeply. Being on the Trail, with its lack of caffeine and sugar, changed all that. Now, even the slightest caffeine or sugar, even hours before bed, would keep me up. So, in town, I would get my sugar cravings out of the way as early as possible and save the veggies and fruits for my night time snacking.

Even though I figured out the proper formula for enjoying a real bed, I rarely stayed more than one night in town. At Shaw's in Monson, Maine I stayed two nights in order to help heal my Achilles. Two nights at The Doyle Hotel in Duncannon, Pennsylvania, while I waited out some bad weather and enjoyed some southbound camaraderie. Two nights at Dave's Place in Damascus, Virginia, in order to catch a ride up to Gettysburg, Pennsylvania, for a conference.

Not counting Amicalola Lodge, AFTER I had completed the AT, the most expensive place I stayed was the Sunset Inn in Hanover, New Hampshire, for $72 a night. The next most expensive, at $70 per night, was the Econo Lodge in Fort Montgomery, New York. Both were located outside of town. In contrast, I stayed at four hostels that were free (all with shower and electricity, some with free laundry). Out of the 136 days I was on the AT I spent 35 nights in a hotel, hostel or campground and 10 nights with friends or family.

15. A Walk in New Jersey

The monument at High Point State Park.

Length:	72 miles	116 km
Max Elevation:	1,685 feet	514 m
Min Elevation:	350 feet	107 m
My First Day:	August 9	
My Last Day:	August 13	

What's it like?

People tend to be a bit incredulous when they learn the AT travels through New Jersey. The Trail actually skirts along the northern border, just a few miles from New York, and even finds itself zigzagging back and forth across state lines. It then travels along the western border before finally crossing in to Pennsylvania. It's almost comical how the Trail is in New Jersey and yet hugs the state border as if it's afraid to fully commit to the relationship.

There's no sign to welcome you to New Jersey, just some graffiti. Or maybe they just had too much white paint left after marking the white blaze on that rock? hehehe

Like New York, the state has some delicious local creameries, along with wild blueberries and blackberries. It continues the tradition established by New York of being a transitional state and contains some varied terrains, including a world class boardwalk through a marsh. And, before you are done with the state, you will find yourself on a very pronounced ridge that will take you into Pennsylvania and offers you some really nice views.

A few highlights

Near Vernon Valley, New Jersey, the AT passes through a marshy floodplain with grasses growing over my head. To allow the trail to traverse this area, a 1.5 mile wooden boardwalk was constructed allowing two or three hikers to walk abreast. The boardwalk sits a foot or two above the marsh and it is quite a unique experience to walk the full length of it.

Part of the 1.5 mile boardwalk in Vernon Valley, taking you through the grassland.

16. Hiking (Concerns)

Have you seen any wildlife?

Have I seen any wildlife? Golly did I ever! Well, not as much as you'd think. The big ones people ask about are moose, bear and rattle snakes - and I consider myself fortunate to have seen some of each.

In Maine I saw three and a half moose, but none had those picturesque racks that exemplify these massive wild cows. The first one I saw was in the 100 Mile Wilderness, just one day outside of Baxter State Park. I was hiking a dozen strides in front of my friend Adam when we spotted a large brown mass just 100 feet ahead on the trail. As Adam was quietly praying that I would get my camera out in time, it calmly and effortlessly walked into the woods a short distance, as if it really didn't care that we were there. I fired off the best picture I could get and was pleased to find out later that you can still identify the silhouette as belonging to a moose, camouflaged amazingly well. Later that day, a fellow that was hiking ahead of us by a few miles excitedly asked "Did you see that moose in the woods near that shelter?" "Yes," I replied, "but it was on the trail when we saw it and moved into the woods." He smiled with amusement, "That's interesting, because it was on the trail when I saw it and it moved off into the woods." Like a costumed performer at Disney World, this moose apparently knew how to thrill tourists.

I knew many thru-hikers that went the whole Trail without seeing a moose, but I did manage to see two more on the trail itself and each one more interested in running away than posing for a photo. Oddly, the moose scat seemed to be covering every square inch of ground in Maine, and yet they were amazingly elusive.

One moose doesn't go in to my tally because I only heard it. Walking up Moxie Bald Mountain, through a thick forest with many downed trees, I heard an enormous crashing sound coming at me like a bus out of control in the woods. I couldn't see very far due to the terrain, and didn't know exactly where it was, so I simply shouted "Hey MOOSE, I'm HERE, hey MOOSE!" For a split second the breaking of branches, crumpling of leaves and snapping of saplings stopped and I imagined it trying to decide what to do next. At this time, brief though it was, I hoped it wasn't a bear stopping to figure out how best to eat me. Then the solitary stampede changed directions and was now moving away from me across the mountain side and into silence.

The 3.5th (3rd and a half?) moose I saw was unfortunate to have been scared into the Mahoosuc Notch. The Mahoosuc Notch is one of the fabled regions spoken of in hushed whispers by frightened Northbounders. I'm being sarcastic, but the truth is that many hikers will claim that the Mahoosuc Notch is physically the hardest place on the trail. It's certainly one of the most memorable. At only 50 to 100 feet wide this is where two mountains form a valley and the rubbled collapse of one mountain has filled the valley floor with small to bus-sized boulders requiring you to not so much hike as rock scramble. You might have to remove your pack and slide it behind you as you crawl through a small gap under 50 tons of Mother Nature's bricks. I thought this was a blast and not at all difficult, although admittedly most of the complaints are probably from the uphill climb out of the notch - which is downhill and far easier for Southbounders.

Anyway, about four days before I came to the notch there was a moose enjoying some tasty grass near the edge of the boulder field when several hikers (not thru-hikers) decided they wanted to get a better angle on their photograph. Spooked by the movement, the moose ran into the notch rather than towards the safety of the woods. The hikers pursued to get that elusive perfect photo. Moving just 50 feet further in to the notch it stumbled and fell in to a crevice, breaking its leg and injuring its head and neck. Over the next few days it thrashed so much that its rack fell off in pieces and was never able to free itself. The Department of Fish and Wildlife was called to put it down, but because the animal was too far from road access they had to deny the request. Even with only 50 feet of space on either side, it was actually possible to blaze a trail such that you could miss the site if you didn't know where to look. When I passed through, the moose was dead, killed that morning by a compassionate person or by natural causes (rumors abound for either scenario), and already there were branches placed at the top of the crevice to give it some privacy and alert hikers to the detour. When I reached the end of the notch there was a man sitting with a sidearm holstered on his belt. "Did you come to put the moose out of its misery?" I asked. "I did, but it was already dead when I got here." I didn't inquire further, but from the gun he looked like an off duty police officer.

I had expected to see black bear in Maine and New Hampshire, but I didn't. The first bear I saw was in Vermont and I jokingly say "I ran into it" because of the circumstances. At the Happy Hill Shelter I was staying with another Southbounder and a Northbounder. The latter told us that 2.5 miles away *in* Podunk Brook was a collection of Gatorade, soda, water and beer for us to enjoy in the morning. Rather than wait till then, I decided to take drink orders and run down to play bartender. About a mile into the run I passed through an isolated meadow and back into the trees on the other side. One hundred yards later as I rounded a bend I looked up to see a large black ball of fur about 20 feet in front of me and closing. Before I could grind my heels to a halt, and without even turning to see what I was, the yearling (in between cub and full size adult) simply jumped to all fours and took off running away from me. I skidded to a halt, grabbed a branch and for the next 1.5 miles I was singing loudly and dragging a stick (for noise) as I ran. At the stream I grabbed a beer, two Mountain Dews and a Gatorade. On the way back I continued to sing and drag my stick but never saw it again.

Continuing with tradition, the next time I saw a black bear I was also running. An hour before sunset, while preparing dinner at the Tom Leonard Shelter in Massachusetts, a Northbounder entered camp and vaguely asked if I had a tarp. I responded that I had one for my shelter and stared blankly at him, thinking it odd that he'd start a conversation this way. Looking at my rain fly he says "Oh, anything stronger? There's a day-hiker that needs it to carry her dog." Not expecting this response, I pry for more information, "Tarp aside, does she need help?" Joining forces with a Northbounder, we go into MacGyver-mode and grab anything we think could be helpful, not knowing what to expect - we had no idea what kind of dog or how injured it was. I grab some rope and a jacket to construct a stretcher; someone grabs a flashlight and water bottle. As we are running at an easy pace along a steep and rocky hillside, we spot two yearlings a couple hundred feet away at the base of the hill, just as they decide to flee from us noisy humans. When we reach the hiker with her adult German Shepherd, we grab two long branches and use the jackets to construct a basic stretcher. The dog has heat-stroke and can't even stand up, it hardly even moves as we pick it up to lower it on to the stretcher. Just as the sun is hitting the horizon, our dog rescue party arrives back at the shelter, which is still a mile from the nearest road. At this late hour it's too far to tackle safely. As a result of a few cell phone calls, the dog and owner rendezvous with a few friends who hike up to help out and bring supplies to make the night more bearable. By morning, the dog has recovered nicely and while it requires frequent breaks and encouragement it makes it to the car without being carried. I have continued to maintain contact with the dog owner and am pleased to say that all these months later the dog is still happy and healthy. The owner even completed her own southbound hike in 2008!

I was told odds were good I'd see bear in Connecticut and the chances were 100% of seeing some in New Jersey. Connecticut, New York and New Jersey for me were void of any sightings and it wasn't until Shenandoah National Park in northern Virginia that I got my due. And boy did I. Of the four days I was in the park I saw a mix of adults, cubs and yearlings, totaling an even dozen. On my third day, I was walking along the trail when I was abruptly halted by a small branch falling a few feet in front of me. I laughed at the thought of Mother Nature playing a joke on me when I casually looked up to see, just ten feet above my head, a young black bear frozen in fear, staring down at me. With the same look on my own face, I had the feeling we were both thinking "Oh crud, what now? Should I run? Should I let it run?" Our stalemate ended as I instinctively chose to walk briskly ahead. When I had put 50 feet between us, I turned around and saw the yearling still frozen in place, perched on the branch, hoping that if it stayed completely still maybe I wouldn't see it.

Berry season had passed and the food of choice for bears was now the acorn, which is why that yearling was in the tree (an acorn grocery store). This was also evident on one other occasion in the park. After a 45 minute nap near a picnic ground parking lot, I headed back to the trail, only to find a group of people excitedly staring up at the top of a tree. There, at the edge of the parking lot, in the canopy of a 100 foot tall tree, directly above a white Subaru station wagon, was a large mother and her two cubs. The cubs were both asleep, slumped over a branch, occasionally shifting or stretching. Mom was busy grabbing at branches, pulling the acorns closer and completely ignoring the seven of us below her. Defying all odds, the matriarch would walk around the tree top on branches seemingly too small for her immense size. She would stand with one rear leg on a thick branch, straddling open space to another branch and with both arms in front of her she'd reach out several feet to pluck at an appealing bunch of nuts, often holding on in order to support herself. I knew bears could climb trees, I didn't know they could nimbly clamber in the canopy as surely as if they were on the ground.

The nine other bears I saw in Shenandoah were far more interested in running away from me than hanging around to see what I'd do. Some were on the trail in front of me, the rest were off in the woods nearby. On one occasion, I startled a cub as I rounded a corner and it immediately climbed up a tree a short distance from the trail. Instantly I realized that mom must be around and she'll soon be very unhappy with me for being so close, so I turned and quickly backtracked. After waiting five minutes and singing loudly all the while, I came back down the trail to find it void of any wildlife and safe for my passage.

Outside Shenandoah, in the 700 or so miles remaining, I only saw one other bear, also in Virginia, who was quick to run away.

The Smoky Mountains were supposed to have a lot of them, but they must have been on vacation. There were occasionally signs posted about "problem bears" that no longer feared humans and would come into a shelter at night to grab a food bag or backpack. Stalking, while still rare, was more common than I'd expect and involves a bear calmly following you until you get scared and throw food or leave your pack. This is probably a learned behavior resulting from one too many scared hikers hoping to appease a bear by throwing their lunch at it.

I did see four rattlesnakes and almost stepped on two of them before I had the sense to jump far out of the way. As snakes tend to do, rattlers can often be found sunning themselves in the middle of the trail all stretched out and quiet. When aggravated they will coil up and shake their rattle, sometimes rattling even as they slowly slither off the trail. I'm not aware of anyone being bitten this year, but I did hear about a thru-hiker whose dog was bitten in the face and had to receive treatment. Black rat snakes were more common and nothing at all to worry about. While still poisonous, these amazingly long and deeply black snakes are more interested in

An eastern rattlesnake on the trail in Virginia. It rattled at me for a few minutes before deciding to slide off the trail - rattling while it slithered.

rats and small prey. It's still very startling to come upon one and realize it at the last second.

I saw a fox in Shenandoah during the day, a rare event, and of course lots of deer all over the trail. I never saw raccoons, opossum, or skunks. The first time I crossed a cow pasture was a bizarre feeling and one I became numb to as time went by. I did cross a field where all the cows got worked up over my presence and began chasing me as only a cow could. Two were actually running (jogging) while a dozen others were jogging (walking fast) to catch me. They weren't bulls at least, so I wasn't exactly scared, but they also weren't milking cows desperate for a squeeze, so I really have no idea why they were after me. I imagined myself getting trampled and thought it best not to find out what their intentions were, so I hurried over to the forested section of the pasture and moved along the tree line to the exit. Of the 20 or so herds I'd come in contact with none had responded this way. In hindsight I feel like a dweeb - frightened by cows.

But there is one cow pasture on the Trail where I feel caution is warranted. Going up and over Hump Mountain Bald means walking through a very large pasture where you will find long-horned cattle grazing contently. When I passed through, there were three males, two of which had horns about four feet from tip to tip while the head honcho's set had to be six feet in overall length and his muscular neck could put an oak tree to shame. Even though I trusted the ATC's decision to put the trail here, and knowing that thousands hike through every year, I still wanted to give these guys a very wide berth - as the males stared me down from 200 feet away.

No AT hike would be complete without the wild ponies of Grayson Highlands, a very special treat indeed. I pretty much lived in Virginia for seven years and I didn't even know we had wild ponies in the state anywhere other than Assateague Island, where they're a big tourist attraction. Grayson Highlands alone is a spectacular and beautiful range of forest, mountain and grassland, but the biggest reason for the popularity is these miniature horses that roam free and hardly seem to mind sharing the land with hikers. Every year, to manage the population, the ponies are rounded up to have a portion sold off. I passed through the area in October just after a round-up and, while they were definitely wary of me, they didn't seem bothered by my presence - at least not as long as I was 20 feet away.

Have you had any problems?

In my final days of employment I was asked in a company meeting if I was worried I might get hurt. I replied that I wished I would be so lucky, for it wouldn't be much of an adventure if there wasn't adversity. Bam! Right there I jinxed myself! Along these lines I had such an uneventful trip that normally mundane and insignificant events are now upgraded to "problem" status. There was only one instance of what would actually be correctly classified as an injury, and that was to my Achilles Heel.

My Achilles

On the first day in the 100 Mile Wilderness, I was carrying nearly 35 pounds on my back and I weighed 175 pounds, so my legs were supporting 210 pounds at each step, something they were definitely not used to doing. Adam and I were pushing ourselves in the 100 Mile Wilderness, tackling several 20 plus mile days in fickle terrain and even though we were quickly lightening our loads by eating two to three pounds of food each day, it was still enough stress to tear, or at least pull, my Achilles tendon. It screamed in pain with each uphill step, no matter what the incline, and it took two weeks until the pain began to subside and a month for it to disappear.

My feet

I've always had fickle feet, which is why I almost exclusively wore very flat, wide, indoor soccer shoes growing up. I knew this was going to be an issue for me on the Trail, even with properly broken-in and seemingly comfortable lightweight hiking shoes. The problem I ran into was with the insoles that I chose after field

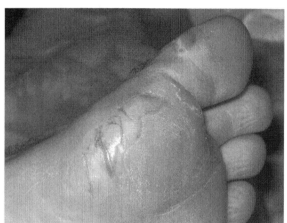

My feet were cracking apart from all the rain in New England.

testing and comparing several types. The shoes performed admirably, the insoles, however, caused bad blisters on my arches that I was able to prevent with different insoles (and for a time no insole at all). But just then I was hitting several weeks worth of perpetual New England rain and it prevented my feet from healing. Furthermore, the rain eroded all my protective calluses, a problem that would come back to haunt me later.

I could have lived with the shoes and the condition of my feet, but sustained rain would occasionally cause the tops of my swollen toes to be rubbed raw by my wet shoes. Because of this, at the halfway mark I decided to experiment with Chaco hiking sandals and socks, which, I have to say, was the perfect footwear for me! What I didn't realize until it was too late was that the extra air flow would dry out my feet - normally not a big deal except it caused what was left of my calluses to crack, resulting in considerable discomfort. In North Carolina, I suddenly noticed that I had been subconsciously walking for a few days on the toes of one foot and the heel of the other, in order to avoid direct pressure to the cracks. I began a regimen of foot crèmes and balms that made things tolerable, but it still took a month after the end of the Trail for my feet to return to a reasonably normal state.

The cold

I got lucky with the weather, and it's not safe to rely on luck. Towards the end of my trip, as I approached the Smoky Mountains, the temperature was dropping. I was forever wondering if I should have more clothing and a warmer sleeping bag sent from my Base Camp. Maybe even a rain coat. Temperatures at night were falling below 40°F for the first time. While I just barely had the gear to handle that, if it was combined with rain I could easily have fallen victim to hypothermia. But I gambled and was fortunate that rain and cold temperatures didn't coincide. Even still, one day I spent two hours in a brick

My coldest night (35°F) was just north of the Smokies. I had to get inventive to stay warm. By 8am it had warmed to 38°F, according to this thermometer I found at a parking lot.

and cement parking lot privy trying to warm up and then proceeded to stomp around the parking lot for another hour to thaw out my sandaled feet. And yes, even in the cold I was still wearing my Chaco sandals.

Just like in New Hampshire, my theory was that if I ever was too cold and/or wet I could wait out the weather in the warmth of my sleeping bag. Fortunately, it never came to that.

Water

Drought has been mentioned before, so I won't go into too much detail here. I will say that it wasn't uncommon to carry upwards of seven liters of water in the second half of the Trail - enough for one and a half days or 30 miles. In contrast, I spent most of the first half carrying only two liters.

Diarrhea

Worried about a contaminated water source and/or improper water treatment, somehow I found myself talking about bowel issues with a fellow hiker. We had been having the same problem for the same amount of time and with the same progression of symptoms. The symptoms included unexpected and more frequent bowel movements (thankfully I was carrying a camp shovel for just such occasions). Our concern was that we probably drank from the same water source since we'd been traveling together for a while and neglected to treat it properly. Based entirely on verbal diagnosis, a doctor in town decided it could be Giardia and put me on antibiotics. The next day I started feeling better - but the same was true for my companion who was not on any medication. Over the next week our conditions improved at the same rate, leading me to believe that Giardia was not the correct diagnosis. In hindsight, I'm still glad I erred on the side of caution.

I learned later that it's quite common to have these symptoms after eating at your first all-you-can-eat buffet. Your body isn't used to consuming that many calories so quickly and it basically goes into food poison mode. This diagnosis would make sense since we had both eaten at our very first buffet together – the other person at the buffet with us did not have these symptoms so it seems actual food poisoning is unlikely to be the cause.

How were the bugs?

I pretty much had a miserable time with mosquitoes from Maine to Connecticut, with the occasional moment of relief in windy, rainy, or high elevation areas. They were vicious and annoying.

I had a few weapons at my disposal to help fend off the little buggers. Long sleeves, pants and a hat were the primary line of defense and the most environmentally friendly. While fairly successful, the heat of summer made this option almost as annoying as the insects.

The 98% DEET chemical bug repellent I used worked amazingly well, but it's such nasty stuff I tried to avoid it. At the start of mosquito season, in the Adirondack Mountains of New York, I went for a day-hike in swamp country. For the first third of my hike, I wore long sleeves to see how well that worked, and then I switched to short sleeves, and finally DEET. Long sleeves were very effective, short sleeves turned me in to a proboscis pin-cushion, and the DEET made me invisible (just as effective as long sleeves). In the end, I wore them when I could tolerate it, then switched to short sleeves and only used the DEET when the biting became too much.

As much as I hate to say it, DEET is a necessary part of a hiker's toolkit if you're in mosquito country at the wrong time of year. You might not want to use it, you might try not to use it, but there are just some moments when the biting becomes too much. While in motion you're probably OK, but then you stop for lunch and your neck, hands, ears, forehead and cheek become big beacons to those little biters and you practically go insane. A little dab of DEET will do ya and in no time flat they're hovering around your clothing but avoiding your skin. Unfortunately you'll then discover that the shirt, pants, socks and hat you're wearing are not impenetrable and you'll jump up from your lunch and just eat on the go. DEET will erode plastics so I don't recommend prolonged use of it on your synthetic clothing - but again desperate times call for desperate measures. I spent one night in a shelter in Vermont and I hardly slept due to the constant biting - and while I could have put a hat over my face that would have just annoyed me in a different way.

Black flies were a big concern, but I managed to avoid the brunt of their force. In all of Maine I only once found them to be problematic and it was in only one small campground. In Massachusetts and Connecticut, they would come out around dinner time and force me into my hammock where I'd learn that they can easily bite through hammock material AND a silk sleeping bag liner (at which point I'd use my sleeping pad even though it kept me too warm). Here and there in Pennsylvania I'd have to put up with them again but to a far lesser degree.

Most annoying though were the little anonymous guys that kept buzzing my ears, face and calf muscles. The solution was actually pretty simple. Pick up any random stick that you can comfortably hold in front of your face and randomly alternate it from ear to ear. For some reason these things don't understand where you are anymore and they leave you alone. If you feel something buzzing around your calf looking for a chance to bite, just give that stick a few swings behind you. The stick technique made me look like a goofball, I'm sure, but it was the cheapest and most environmentally friendly solution I found. I carried a stick like this all over the AT and for probably 1,000 miles total. At times it had leaves on it, at other times it was barren, but it was always light and disposable.

I also discovered that strategically placing large leaves in your hat so that they come down and cover your ears and even over your eyebrows can be amazingly effective at keeping bugs from giving you fly-bys.

Finding ways to keep annoying insects from buzzing my eyes and ears.

What do you do when it rains?

I get wet when it rains! Rain is just a free shower AND a natural Laundromat. While I did carry a rain jacket for much of the Trail, I never once wore it in the rain. A rain jacket doesn't do you much good if you just end up sweating underneath, so I used mine only in camp/town to keep the bugs off or stay warm. I saw it more as a wind breaker than a moisture barrier.

As soon as the rain came I would generally stop to pull out my backpack cover and maybe grab my hat, just to keep the rain out of my eyes. No need to change footwear because they'll dry fast. No need to change clothes because instead of drenching them in sweat, I'll now be rinsing them off.

The equation gets a little trickier when temperature comes in to play. Most of the time it was hot, so soaking my clothes was welcomed. However, it's both uncomfortable and dangerous to get soaking wet when it's cold out. As long as I was moving I was all right, but if I stopped for lunch, dinner or to camp I could easily start shivering. The idea is pretty simple then: if the temperature is low and I'm soaking wet, keep moving or stop to camp and change into dry clothes. On days like that I would walk straight through lunch and dinner and just eat once I had set up somewhere for the evening.

But wait, there's something missing... ah, yes, the whole "what happens in the morning?" thing. You might be dry and comfy in camp but it's still cold and by morning it will probably be colder. Your clothes are soaked, and they're not going to dry by the time you wake up. Hey, I didn't say the plan was perfect! Unfortunately, this is where you just have to get used to waking up to put on very wet, very cold clothes. Shivering may distract you from being happy, but once you put on your backpack it will help insulate your back and once you start hiking you will warm up. It's best to eat something with a lot of energy to help kick-start your system, too.

This way of dealing with precipitation was almost perfect for me. Things very nearly fell apart when the first frost hit towards the end of my hike and in general temperatures were much cooler. There were times when it was raining and I worried that if the temperature dropped just a few more degrees I'd have been forced to set up camp and wait out the storm (which could require several days for all I knew). Knowing how easily one can become hypothermic, I felt like an idiot for taking such risks in the sometimes remote stretches of the south. Then again, I was looking for some adversity and adventure on the AT, so I can't complain.

There were certainly many hikers who would religiously don their rain jacket, as well as rain pants, at the first sign of precipitation. There were also people that would use an umbrella instead. While I never tried it, I really like this idea. With the exception of a wind and rain mixture, it seems like a very sensible method to hold back Mother Nature. I'd recommend giving the umbrella a try.

"Dogs" vs "Dogs!!!"

Crikey, who knew these cute little canine companions could be the cause of so much controversy!? Yes, there are a good number of dogs on the AT. Yes, there are three places where dogs are not allowed - Smoky Mountains National Park, Baxter State Park, and Bear Mountain Zoo. I saw a lot of dogs and even though I tend to find dogs endearing, I must say that many of them were not well-behaved. You'll hear hikers complain that dogs shouldn't be allowed on the Trail - when in reality their complaints have more to do with bad training than the actual idea of dogs.

For example, you will hear complaints about barking, stealing food, growling and chewing on gear. In my mind, if you want to ban dogs based on training issues, then I'd love to ban people that snore, talk incessantly, smell bad or hog the shelter.

The only logical arguments I came across are that dogs do stir up water sources - especially bad in drought conditions, when a puddle is all you have - and that a good number of people are afraid of dogs. I did find it amusing that for so many people this is the hot issue and that most of them simply don't like dogs. I had just assumed that hikers would generally be "dog people" and have since learned otherwise.

I was particularly thrilled when I came upon a day-hiker with a German Shepherd puppy. Not because the puppy was so cute, but because the hiker asked if I would let his dog smell me and if I would give it a treat. He was training his dog at a young age to behave while hiking and specifically wanted it to be comfortable around thru-hikers, since he intended to thru-hike with his canine in a year or so.

From an owner's perspective, you have to be mindful of the fact that there may be a fair amount of road walking involved that may be hurtful to dog paws, especially if there's broken glass. You also have to be aware that many lodgings don't allow dogs and that certainly many businesses will require you to leave your dog outside.

Apart from companionship, dogs do have the added benefit of security. Wild animals are more likely to stay away (including bears) and the same can be said for unwelcome human contact.

17. A Walk in Pennsylvania

A harvested hay crop in one of the flat sections of Pennsylvania trail.

Length:	230 miles	370 km
Max Elevation:	2,080 feet	634 m
Min Elevation:	320 feet	98 m
My First Day:	August 13	
My Last Day:	August 25	

What's it like?

Reaching Pennsylvania marks an important milestone for a Southbounder for a few reasons: 1. not since Maine have we had a state with so many miles in it, 2. finally we have a state with some very flat and easy sections, 3. now we get to learn if all the Northbounders were lying about how bad the rocks are in Pennsylvania.

Similar in a way to Connecticut, the state can be characterized as "a ridge walk followed by farm land followed by a ridge walk." In Pennsylvania you will find yourself walking along reasonably flat ridges, occasionally broken up by a deep gap, and at the bottom you'll find a river and a major highway. In between the numerous ridges running like train tracks through the state, there are long stretches of very flat, fertile farm lands. Since the AT leaves the state on a different ridge than the one you entered it from, it is necessary to cross a few of these flat stretches.

Pennsylvania has lots of flat walks through corn fields.

The combination of long ridges and long flat valleys means that most people will have their longest mileage days here (this is where I had my first day over 30 miles, but it wasn't my longest). The Pennsylvania locals told me that every year the ridges go in to a drought, and I can confirm that the shelters and sections of trail on the ridges had no running water except for one. In many cases, you would have to walk downhill for a ways before finding water.

For much of the state, I relied on towns or hostels to refill my water bottles. Homes would often have signs posted, informing hikers that they can grab water from a garden hose on the side of the house, or sometimes local business or fire stations would let hikers fill up. At least while crossing the flat valleys, you could often find a stream or river.

For a while now, Pennsylvania has also played host to the official mid-point marker of the Trail in and/or near Pine Grove Furnace State Park (depending on what year you hike it). For the year 2000, an actual marker in the form of a tall wooden pole with signs (it looks somewhat artistic) was erected, but it is basically only accurate for that year. For other years, you just have to rely on your guidebook and an imagination.

Along the Trail there is a lot of mining history. There are sections that were once forested, but now not even weeds are growing (Lehigh Gap) due to heavy metal contamination. There

The half-way point marker for the year 2000.

The famous Reading Railroad depot and museum (closed for the day when I arrived).

is a ghost town (Rausch Gap) where once there was a flourishing coal mine town. On the flip side of that coin there is Reading, Pennsylvania (where Monopoly gets its Reading Railroad), which was famous for its anthracite mining and railroad distribution – Reading was successfully converted into a tourist destination and the railway station is now a museum.

Pennsylvania is also known for being the first state where a Southbounder is likely to see an eastern rattlesnake. As for flora, while there are rhododendrons the full length of the Trail, it's in Pennsylvania where a Sobo will first encounter a growth so dense and lengthy that you'll lose all sight of the trees beyond and the sun will nearly disappear. Patches like this are common throughout the rest of the Trail heading south.

It's also the source of the "Half Gallon Challenge", in Pine Grove Furnace State Park. Having reached the half way point, hikers can buy a half gallon of any ice cream at the park concession stand. If they can finish the whole thing in less than an hour, they receive a prized wooden spoon. Special notice is given, by way of a photograph at the register, to the hiker that does it in the fastest time. I'm told the trick is to allow the ice cream to melt and then drink it. It seems most of the hikers I spoke to that tried this challenge ended up getting sick or at least carrying an upset stomach for a while.

In our typically conservative Southbounder nature, four of us opted to try our own version of the event, which I dubbed the "Two Scoop Challenge" – this was guaranteed to produce winners and no upset tummies! Since it was near the end of the summer, there also weren't that many flavor options left if you wanted a half gallon - just vanilla and chocolate.

A few highlights

I arrived at Rausch Gap near sunset on a cold August 19, and there was an eerie darkness to the woods, made more so by the presence of various old foundations, walls and stone piles. Rausch Gap was once a thriving coal mine town with 1,000 residents in 1860, 100 in 1875 and by 1910 there were no more people and the buildings were torn down. The woods have reclaimed the land and you'd never know it was such a populated place. The cemetery side trail is a big highlight for hikers, but due to fatigue, darkness, and lack of water, I and my fellow hikers decided to head straight for the shelter.

The Hawk Mountain Sanctuary (near Port Clinton, Pennsylvania) consists of trails for all skill levels and a large population of hawks to keep the bird watchers happy. The AT is placed perfectly through this park, giving you secluded forest, sweeping views, and the occasional public restroom. The AT doesn't hit all the great views the sanctuary has to offer, so you can definitely take your time to throw in side trips and loops.

Just before entering the Hawk Mountain Sanctuary area is the free-for-hikers Eckville Shelter. The house next door was donated to the AT and the shelter is maintained by the caretaker living in the house. The shelter has a small library, board games and several comfortable bunks.

The state maintains several quirky shelters. One campground has shelters labeled "His" and "Hers," another has "Snoring" and "Non-Snoring" lean-tos and this one is designed to look like an old inn. White-washed plaster, potted plants and brass lanterns complete the look.

18. Socializing

How does information travel?

If I ever mentioned in conversation that I knew where some friends were behind me, the natural response would be "How do you know who's behind you?" Often you only know information about what (or who) is in front of you, and since that's the easier question to answer I'll tackle that first.

Along the Trail, you will periodically find something called a register or log book. A register is usually just a large spiral notebook but can sometimes take the form of more expensive leather-bound ledgers. Almost every shelter and hostel has a register but they can also be found sprinkled throughout the Trail, attached to signs or their own dedicated mailbox-like structure. Normally a pen will be provided, and since most hikers carry writing implements, you just might find an extra one waiting around for the original to run out of ink.

Hikers use these notebooks for anything from a simple signature (letting others know they were there) to a nine page story about how they spent their day. You will find complaints, praises, poems, art work, puzzles and even magazine cutouts taped to a page. Apart from entertainment, these registers can also serve to inform hikers about the trail ahead, such as water sources, detours, wildlife, hornet nests and ground bees, hostel or motel information or the local weather.

Registers are, therefore, very useful, but they still can't tell you where your fellow hikers are behind you. For that you need technology or luck. Luck, for instance, can happen when you meet a day- or section-hiker that just happened to be hiking a section of trail behind you, they run into some thru-hikers, and then they run in to you in town on their way home. I had walked with, and subsequently moved past, several Southbounders with whom I exchanged email or cell phone numbers and I would occasionally talk with or email them. Since a lot of people update websites with information about their hike, that was another way of digging up news.

My news source was often non-thru-hikers who happened to meet some of my fellow hikers on another part of the trail days, weeks or even months prior. I could end up in a hostel only to have someone tell me they were day-hiking a few weeks ago when they ran into So-and-So. Three months into my trip I met a group who happened to be camping near Springer Mountain in Georgia with some Northbounders. I happened to spend a few days with those very same Northbounders at a hostel way back in Maine.

What's your Trail name?

The topic of Trail names either gets me in trouble or it gets laughs. Let's start at the beginning. A tradition was born a long time ago of hikers taking on nicknames and now it's generally assumed that every hiker will have one. Some say you have to be given your name, while others prefer to assign it themselves, for fear of receiving something less than ideal.

When I started the Trail, I wasn't sure if I wanted a nickname and figured I would simply let fate take care of it. In the 100 Mile Wilderness, three days into my journey, fate indeed grabbed hold and made it clear that Trail names weren't for me. At a crowded shelter I met a lady who introduced herself as "Clique" (not her real nickname); I responded with "Hi, I'm Ken and this is my friend Adam." She froze, not sure what to say next and looking as if I just slapped her. I don't recall the exact exchange that followed, but it involved her not knowing how to talk to me since I didn't have a Trail name, then confusion as she tried to figure out why I didn't have one, then rejection as she walked off clearly not wanting anything to do with us.

It felt like I was just rejected from a high school clique. I didn't want to be called "Gargantua the Free" or "Agile Toes" if it meant having to join some elitist social club known as "Thru-Hiker."

The problem was I really started to hate the responses I'd get. "Hi, I'm Ken and this is Adam" would always be followed with a subtle look of confusion and then disbelief and "What, no Trail name?!?!?!?!"

And so it was that, four days into my hike, I decided Adam and I would follow the rules - he christened me "Kenneth" while I ordained him "Adam" and from there on out I would almost always say "I'm Kenneth, and yes, that's my Trail name" or "My real name is Ken, my Trail name is Kenneth."

I was bucking the system intentionally and some insightful people would comprehend this and laugh, while congratulating me on this new take on tradition. Others would just look confused and take pity on me while trying to assign me a proper name. Out of desperation, I did allow one person to call me "Rum Cake," as long as it made her feel better but I warned her I'd deny any knowledge of the nickname. A few people I'd hiked with in Maine, and formed a good friendship with, independently came up with a Trail name of "The Big K," in reference to the fact that while all the Northbounders are "chasing Katahdin, the big K" these Southbounders were chasing me... which was arguably more fun than chasing Springer Mountain.

In the summer of 2009, I took a motorcycle ride through Shenandoah and stopped for a milkshake at a camp store. Relaxing outside was a fellow that looked like a thru-hiker, so I stop to chat him up and we talk about the Trail. He asks me what my Trail name was, so I reply with "Kenneth." His face ripe with excitement, he replies "I remember you, you idiot, you never got a Trail name!?" It turns out he's a ridge runner - someone that is paid to informally police sections of the AT for the summer - and I had met him in New Jersey while hiking in 2007. He also made fun of me then for not having a nickname... but at least he remembered my name!

Enough of me being a spoil-sport; let's explore this phenomena. Trail names can be mundane, creative, obvious, or completely random and I'd categorize them in this way (all names are made up to protect the innocent):

Fun

Having a nickname is a conversation starter, an ice breaker, a way of breaking free from the norm and shaking up reality. Many people like the idea of escaping from the cage that had become their life, and they do so with sometimes ludicrous sounding names. "Hi, I'm The Left Sandal of Jesus."

Alter Ego

I had heard about people on the Trail, past and present, who took this concept to a whole other level. Starting with a Trail name, they would build themselves an entirely new persona, complete with a fabricated past and convince people they were this entirely other person. It is like going under cover, with a dossier explaining your alternate identity. Except, apart from simply having fun at others expense or living out some fantasy, I'm not really sure of the motivation. To my knowledge I never met anyone hiking the AT this way, but then again, how would I even know? Was Brit's accent fake???

Safety

Trail names are often adopted in order to mask one's true identity, thereby gaining some personal security. Jane might feel more comfortable signing shelter registers as "Bubba Ho Tep" because then there's no sug-gestion that she's female and will feel some measure of security that way. While I'm sure this can be the case, I didn't meet anybody who wanted a name primarily for this reason; although I'm sure on more than one occa-sion it could come in handy.

Several times I wished I had a nickname. As an example, let's say I met an obnoxious hiker a few miles outside of town who is very clingy, spooky and desperate for conversation (there were a good number of these types out there) and I introduce myself as "Achilles." When I get to town, I check in to one motel out of many but I've signed the hiker book with "Kenneth" and checked in with "Ken Sarzynski." Mr. Obnoxious will have no easy way of tracking me down.

99.9% of the time I felt completely safe on the AT, but you never know who might be out there. To that end, since my real name was my Trail name, every time I signed a motel/inn/hostel guest book any anonymity I had was lost. If everyone knew me as Achilles and I signed a motel guest book as Kenneth Sarzynski, they wouldn't associate the two. But if someone signs in as Ken or Kenneth Sarzynski, and all along the Trail people had met me as Kenneth, it's pretty easy to make the connection and then BAM, they now know my full name.

To me, a security concerned computer geek, letting so many strangers know my last name (especially such a unique last name) can put me at risk. With that knowledge they can find my personal website and blog for the AT and with that they know where I am on the Trail or even maybe my home address. Like I said, 99.9% of the time I wouldn't care who has this level of familiarity with my hike, but it's still something to think about.

Hubris

I think a lot of hikers give themselves names that make them feel good. Whether it's pride about your home and you call yourself "Wisconsin" or you just feel like being a braggart and you're known as "Invincible," the names chosen often reflect an inner personality. But of course there are plenty of people on the other end of this spectrum, like "Trash bag" or "Filthy."

Observation

There's a class of names that's easy to understand and doesn't need much coverage. "Baseball Hat," "Red Flag," "Chaco" and so on. The first one wears a baseball hat, the second carries a red flag and the third wears Chaco sandals. Catch my meaning?

But it doesn't have to be so obvious either. "Rum Cake" meant absolutely nothing to anyone, except the one hiker I told about the rum-filled fruit cakes I make for Christmas. A name like "Tide," perhaps, because someone always seems to use Tide laundry detergent.

Tradition

People are often raised to see tradition as something you can't question or deviate from - doing so would incur the wrath of society or family.

Of course you'll have a nickname when you hike the AT, everyone does, there's no question about it!

AT as a social experience

I only started to hear "You should slow down, the AT is about people," when I hit the south (southern Virginia, North Carolina, Tennessee and Georgia). I actually got into an argument with a drunk (among other altered states) man in his 50's over this, and since he worked at outfitters in Tennessee for much of his life, he claimed to be an expert on thru-hiking. At 20-30 miles a day, he said I was going too fast, that I couldn't possibly be enjoying the Trail, and that the miles I was doing were far above normal. Ignoring the fact that he had never attempted a thru-hike (and therefore had no first-hand experience), I realized very quickly that his memory was limited entirely to conversations with Northbounders, who had only been hiking for 340 miles at this point and were generally not in as good a shape as an 1,830 mile Southbounder.

Claiming that all his northbound buddies were going slow and therefore enjoying the AT more, he failed to understand that by the time they hit 1,800 miles they too would probably be moving at my pace.

Anyway, in terms of slowing down, BAH!, everyone should hike their own hike. Some people aim for fewer miles a day; some people aim for higher but take more days off in town. I might have tried for 20-30 miles each day, but in the end I averaged close to 16 (taking into account my days off). And besides, are you telling me that taking even longer to hike through a non-descript tunnel of trees means you'll enjoy the monotony even more?

Throw aside the argument that going slower somehow means more enjoyment and let's talk about what the Trail means. This gentleman was naturally biased by his encounters with Northbounders into thinking that hiking the AT is a social experience. Given the volume of Northbounders starting out each year from Georgia, it is not uncommon to have over 100 people at a shelter or campground for the first few weeks. Generally speaking, Northbounders are in it for the social experience, either intentionally or accidentally. Many ex-thru-hikers I spoke with made comments along the lines of "Oh yeah, I LOOOOOOVED my thru-hike, it was so much fun! I'm jealous of you; I'd love to do it again. I remember that time in Dalton, at the bar..." and almost every fond memory involved a bar full of hikers, or a shelter full of hikers with pizza and beer, etc.

Southbounders, those huggable introverts, are mostly out there for the outdoors experience and solitude. While in New England, there were occasions when I'd have 20-30 thru-hikers at a shelter, five percent of them southbound. So a Southbounder could be part of the party if they wanted to be, but my impression (from the 30 Sobo's that I passed or knew) is that we wanted little to do with that lifestyle.

Plain and simple, the Trail is what YOU want it to be (within certain limits), and don't go around pretending that your experience is the only right one. For me the Trail was about solitude, for many it's the opposite.

The Trail is about the people

Whether you are looking for solitude or socialization, there is one important aspect of the AT that needs special mention. From Maine to Georgia, you'll meet the most wonderful people running hotels, motels and hostels, or maintaining the trail, or offering shuttle rides. Some are ex-thru-hikers while many simply find themselves living near a trailhead or in a trail town.

Many have been doing it for years and really do personify everything good about the AT. They will go out of their way to help you, offer advice or just be a friend. You will be offered meals and support more times than you can count.

Unfortunately, their kindness is often abused and there's no guarantee from year to year that you'll find them out there. In 2007, a hiker was arrested in New Jersey when locals learned he'd been scamming people since Georgia. His game? He would claim a family member was ill and he needed bus fare to get home, then he would pocket the money and continue hiking. It's risky running a scam on the AT, where communication is exceptional.

Many people become legends that everyone wants to meet and won't forget. They are young, old, married, single, handicapped, poor and wealthy. Every year new hostels are opened up by the next generation of Trail legends, we can only hope they are given a chance to shine and not taken advantage of or disrespected by thru-hikers.

19. A Walk in Maryland

The war correspondents monument in Gathland State Park.

Length:	41 miles	66 km
Max Elevation:	1,880 feet	573 m
Min Elevation:	230 feet	70 m
My First Day:	September 1	
My Last Day:	September 3	

What's it like?

Just over the border from Pennsylvania, Maryland starts with a bang at Pen Mar State Park. The park provides a sweeping view of western Maryland, concessions, restrooms, pavilions, and if you're lucky a wedding or party of some kind where you just might be offered food – at least I can only imagine.

Maryland is the buffer zone between the literal midpoint (southern Pennsylvania) and the psychological midpoint (Harpers Ferry, West Virginia). It's so short that hikers have created the "24 Hour Challenge," whereby participants take it upon themselves to complete the entire 41 miles in less than a 24 hour period. You may find makeshift campgrounds pitched on or near the state border in order to give contestants the best possible chance for success.

It's also part of the "Four State Challenge," the goal of which is to hike in four states in less than a 24 hour period. This isn't much more difficult than the "24 Hour Challenge" when you realize that West Virginia is only 4 flat miles long and Maryland isn't all that difficult.

I wonder if anyone has combined all these challenges to create a "Four State Half Gallon Challenge." I'd certainly hate to be the Southbounder that chugged a half gallon of ice cream and then immediately began jogging for West Virginia.

The Trail in Maryland consists of a lot of ups and ends with a quick drop down to the Potomac River where it follows the C&O Canal. Along the way, you will pass by a short side trail leading to the original, and much more modest, Washington Monument (looks like a 30 foot high honey pot). There is a lot of Civil War history as you approach Harpers Ferry. On the AT you will pass through Gathland State Park where there is a war correspondents monument that, at first glance, looks like the front of a building with the other walls demolished. Further examination reveals there never were any other walls and this stone structure is meant to stand alone.

Much of the Trail is near a major road or highway, and since it's not far to DC and Frederick, Maryland, you can see a good number of weekend warriors. Like Pennsylvania, the water sources may not be the most abundant, but you will likely be able to fill up at park restrooms or hostels.

A few highlights

The Washington Monument and Gathland State Park monuments are really quite interesting and seemingly out of place in the middle of a forested ridge. Either would make for a nice day trip, with a brief out-and-back hike on the AT for exercise.

I'll branch out a little bit and mention the C&O Canal as a highlight, not so much for the few miles you're hiking on it in Maryland, but because the canal itself can be made into a really fantastic hike or bike trip. It is a 184 mile packed earth trail from Cumberland, Maryland, to Washington, DC. The AT follows it from mile 58 to 61 where it leaves the canal behind to enter Harpers Ferry by way of a shared railroad/pedestrian bridge. Every 5-10 miles there are established campgrounds on the canal with old fashioned hand-pump water spigots with potable water (although at some the iron content and color might make you think twice).

The original Washington Monument. Great views from the top.

20. How to Help a Hiker

The Trail provides

The phenomena of "the Trail provides" fascinates me and the many hikers that have witnessed it for themselves. The idea is that on some mystical, magical level there's a force or natural balance that is looking out for you and influencing events.

My first experience with this concept was a Northbounder named Bookworm - coincidentally my first encounter with a Nobo. Bookworm unintentionally acquired a lot of enemies by writing entire Dr Seuss stories on brand new privy walls along the entire AT (although I for one enjoyed reading them). But that's beside the point... what I want to say is that Bookworm went through the 100 Mile Wilderness with the intention of stopping at a private campground about half way to re-supply. He somehow missed the side trail to the camp and didn't realize it until he was well beyond.

Even though he was now short by one and a half days worth of food, he decided not to turn around. Like most thru-hikers after 2,000 miles of walking, he figured he could ration and survive until he reached another store (the next one at Abol Bridge outside Baxter State Park). It wouldn't be easy. On the day his food would run out, he came upon a shelter brimming over with abandoned food! There were Lipton dinners, instant oatmeal, granola, and even some unidentifiable powdery substance (tasted like a drink mix to me). Out of the entire 100 Mile Wilderness, this was the only shelter with any reasonable amount of food in it (most likely dropped to lose weight from heavy packs) and it just happened to come at the right time for Bookworm.

I've always tried to live my life with the expectation that, like the Trail, "life will provide." Not to say that I necessarily believe in fate, or a higher being in control, but that maybe through a complex natural balance everything ultimately makes sense and happens for a reason. I try not to analyze it too much, but suffice it to say that many people have commented on this concept as it relates to the AT.

I met a gentleman in Glencliff, New Hampshire and we talked for a while before going our separate ways and exchanging contact info. He lived near the Trail in Virginia and was just up visiting friends and doing some day hikes. A few weeks later, I was more anxious than normal to get to a town so that I could eat and was drooling over the idea of a Friendly's Restaurant in Bennington, Vermont. I hit the road at 9am, hoping for a quick hitch and stuck out my thumb at the first group of vehicles. The last vehicle in the bunch pulled over to the shoulder and I was shocked to see the gentleman from Glencliff behind the wheel - he was equally shocked. On his long drive back to Virginia, and nowhere near where we met, he just happened to give me a ride in to town. Months later, when I made it to central Virginia, he and his family would treat me to a wonderful dinner and a free bed for the night. Just before leaving Virginia I would take a side-trip up to Gettysburg, Pennsylvania, for a conference, where we would once again shake hands. It all seemed more than a coincidence.

Even getting to Gettysburg was an example of the Trail providing. Since New Hampshire in early July, I had debated whether I should try to attend the conference ("The Gathering" for the Appalachian Long Distance Hikers Association) in early October. Knowing that I'd be in southern Virginia or Tennessee and North Carolina around that time I simply didn't know how I could make it - or if I'd really want to take all that time off from my hike. It just so happened that in Damascus, the town just four miles from the Tennessee and North Carolina border, I met a retired ex-thru-hiker who just happened to be spending a few days in town before heading up to The Gathering. We hit it off, spent a lot of time talking about the AT and he easily convinced me to take some time off to rent bikes and a shuttle service so we could pedal down the Virginia Creeper bike trail. All the while I picked his brain about the conference to see if I really wanted to join him and another hiker for the drive up.

On the one hand it looked like life was trying to tell me to go; on the other hand I was situated nicely in a pocket of hiking solitude where I was two days behind and five days ahead of any other Southbounders. Not seeing the decision clearly, I decided to bring in another factor - the wife. I figured that if she could drive up from DC to Pennsylvania for the conference too, then that would settle the matter - otherwise I'd keep hiking. Well, it turns out that that weekend she volunteered to get out of her apartment so that her housemates could use the space for guests and she would simply crash with friends. Driving up to Pennsylvania was the perfect getaway for her, and that closed the deal for me. The next day, Thursday, three of us were driving up to Gettysburg where we'd be until Sunday.

And it just so happens that, of the next three days south of Damascus, I had planned to stay at two hostels whose owners just happened to be at the conference too. If I had skipped The Gathering, I would have found the hostels temporarily closed or at least not had the full range of amenities. Knowing that I was hoping to stay at those places, the gentleman I drove up with introduced me and my wife to Bob of Kincora Hostel and Scott and Ron of Abby's Place. We all sat together at the opening ceremony that night where Bob and Ron each received an award from ALDHA thanking them for all their work on the AT. My wife turned to me and commented, "Wow, you didn't tell me they were celebrities!" and I had to shrug in ignorance. I had a whole new appreciation for those folks that make up Trail lore, and it felt like more than just coincidence that I had met these individuals who I would soon be seeing again once I returned to the Trail. To that end, when I did make it to Kincora and then Abby's Place, it was like a reunion among friends.

But I also had experiences like those of Bookworm. As background, imagine that for three months I have been craving hot dogs almost every day - don't ask me why, but I did. I'm about to hit the Smoky Mountains and I'm planning on stopping at one of the two hostels/stores just miles from the start of the park. My goal is to buy the bulk of my supplies in Hot Springs, North Carolina and to top off at one of these locations (without doing so I figure I will be short one day's worth of food). The operators of the first hostel I hit, Standing Bear Farm, have left a sign saying they're out and to make myself at home (everything is on the honor system). There's mail in the box suggesting they've been gone more than just a day, and the food supplies are locked away and inaccessible. I decide to press on a few miles to Mountain Moma's Kuntry Store and Bunkhouse (1.3 miles off the trail DOWN a steep dirt road). Looks like I never got the news that Mountain Moma decided to sell off and close down, leaving behind a deserted and empty shell of a house. So I fill up my water bottles from the garden hose and trudge 1.3 miles back up the road.

Putting my complete trust in the Trail I figure I'll either be OK with the food I have or I'll find someone that will feed me. Failing that, I figure I can always hitch the 15 miles to Gatlinburg and check out the "Vegas of the south" (which Northbounders seem to love and locals seem to avoid) if I get desperate.

On my second night in the park I arrived at the Icewater Spring Shelter and find it brimming with weekend hikers. A gentleman is eager to find out if I'm a thru-hiker and when I tell him I am, he immediately offers me the food that he was carrying. It turns out that he's one of a group of Trail Angels that for years, on this weekend in October, have been coming to Icewater Spring Shelter with food just for Southbounders. As luck would have it, he had set aside two huge Polish hot dogs, cheese, onions, relish, ketchup and mustard in anticipation of my arrival!!! They even stoked up the fire for me and provided a stick for cooking the dogs. By not having to eat dinner from my own supply, I now felt confident I had enough food to get me through the park. There was also the added benefit that he fulfilled one of my biggest cravings! It's not just hindsight,

Icewater Spring Shelter where some friendly weekend campers treated me to some grilled hot dogs.

but I can honestly say I felt something like this would happen when I left those two hostels empty handed.

Then there are the more isolated experiences. The German bonfire artist I shared a campground with had never been allergic to bee stings, suddenly finds he's dangerously allergic. His body is covered with hives in five minutes, he's feverish, his tongue swells, his lips and cheeks numb, his breathing rapid. Luckily, this is one of those rare occasions that I have cell phone reception, even though we're miles from a road, so I call a friend to do some digging online to see what I should do. My basic first aid knowledge is insufficient for this extreme a reaction. Fortunately I'm carrying Benadryl (I didn't find many other hikers who did) and administer it while I'm waiting for my friend's input. In the end I tell him to lie down, we elevate his stung leg, put a cold cloth over the stings, give him a second Benadryl tablet, and monitor his condition. He said that if he was alone he would have probably tried to hike down to the nearest road, so he wouldn't pass out in the woods alone. Since I was there, AND I had a cell phone, AND the Benadryl seemed to slow the progression of his symptoms, AND I could be there to monitor his condition, he was able to recover at a relaxed pace. By morning he only had hives.

The perfect gift

Thru-hikers will often be asked the question "Do you need anything?" or "Is there anything I can do to help?" You will hear it in town, on the Trail or just hanging around camp. Maybe you have a friend hiking the AT and you're meeting him to camp for a night or two and you want to know what you can bring him.

We're a very simple bunch to please, we truly are. It doesn't take much money, time or consideration.

Food storage bags of all sizes
Useful for storing food, trash, restaurant leftovers and drink mixes, any closable plastic storage bag will do. All it takes is the trash from one tuna package to permanently ruin a Ziploc, so we tend to go through a

good number of them. And while it's easy to buy new ones, we can't justify buying a box of 50, just to use five.

Take my trash, please!

It's a nuisance to have to carry our trash, even if it's not that much. It's stinky, the smell can attract animals, if the garbage bag we're using rips it will get that stink all over our pack, and it's extra weight/bulk we would rather not have to deal with. Normally we have to wait till we hit town to dispose of the trash, but often times there are parks that have garbage cans available for hikers.

Fruits and vegetables without the commitment

If I was at a shelter and someone offered me fresh fruit or vegetables, I would gladly eat all they had. But because they're so heavy, they're not something I could easily justify carrying (although I usually managed) and their nutritional value is one that most hikers could benefit from. In contrast, offer me some instant mashed potatoes or Ramen noodles at a shelter and watch for my carefully concealed cringe.

21. A Walk in West Virginia

Elevated railroad tracks in Harpers Ferry a short distance from the AT.

Length:	4 miles	6 km
Max Elevation:	1,200 feet	366 m
Min Elevation:	265 feet	81 m
My First Day:	September 3	
My Last Day:	September 5	

What's it like?

Short and quick, but jammed full of important sites and historical significance, the West Virginia portion of the AT consists of a walk through historic Harpers Ferry, a bridge over a river and a brief uphill hike to the Virginia border. Blink and you could miss the whole state.

But Harpers Ferry is not to be missed, and as the psychological mid-point of the AT, it is one of the most looked forward to sections. Here you will find the super friendly office of the Appalachian Trail Conservancy, the folks responsible for the Trail, where you can relax and flip through (or now with the use of a computer) old photo albums to see hikers as far back as the 90's on the AT. Before the ATC "went digital" you could count on a Pola-roid picture being taken. Each photo was marked with a color to indicate thru-hiker direction (north or south) or to indicate a section hiker, along with information about you: when you started, optional contact info, age,

A view of the Shenandoah River from Harpers Ferry.

and so forth. I'm sure the process is still the same even though they are now digital.

I spent an hour there, looking over old photos, especially interested in what thru-hikers were wearing and carrying in the 90's. There were a lot of full leather hiking boots, button-down shirts, jean shorts, and metal external frame backpacks (not quite so different from today's external frame packs). I also spent time looking at the photos of Southbounders ahead of me, to finally see what they looked like, after having read their log entries at shelters for so many miles. Lastly, I looked at the Northbounder photos to smile and say "Hey, I remember passing him!"

And yet, Harpers Ferry isn't an ideal hiker town. Stores close early, restaurants aren't open past 8pm, and while there is one super outfitter, there is no place to resupply your food. After checking in to the Hilltop House Hotel, with a few hikers I ran into that day (having last seen them in New Hampshire!), we went in search of food. The local bar was closing up and told us we'd have to walk 1.5 miles out of town to a place called "Pub" if we wanted food. Fortunately, Pub was next to a 7-Eleven, which was the only place within walking distance to buy groceries (yes, I call granola bars, cans of tuna and pretzels "groceries"). Many hikers staying over in Harpers Ferry will end up taking a taxi or hitchhiking the eight miles to Charles Town where you'll find the typical big box stores and chains.

There is a lot to do here, if you're interested in a layover. Whitewater outfitters surround the town and provide trips on the Shenandoah River, or even rent bikes to ride any of the 184 mile C&O Canal. If you want to visit DC or Pittsburgh, you can hop on an Amtrak train right in town.

A few highlights

Harpers Ferry itself is a national historic park, which is why the stores and restaurants close so early. Buildings can be dated back to the late 1700's and are all situated on the slopes of the hillside leading down to the converging Potomac and Shenandoah rivers. Civil war battles were fought on the hillsides surrounding the town and in the town itself. Monuments, old foundations and reconstructed buildings pepper the area. The actual town itself is very small, with only a few restaurants and shops, but it bleeds in to the neighboring town of Bolivar, where more modern residential communities exist.

A view of the river from Harpers Ferry.

22. Health

Where do you go to the bathroom?

Whenever someone asked me how I went to the bathroom, I had to remind myself that some people have never camped or gone for a hike in their life. Most of the time this question is directed more towards the, umm, solid end of the digestive spectrum, and less often it entails, umm, a more fluid conversation.

Let me remind you that hiking the AT is largely about freedom from civilization - and the topic of bodily functions is no exception. That said there are definitely some rules one should follow when considering where to find relief.

A privy typically consists of a hole in the ground upon which a wooden outhouse is built. Many are simply a faithful reconstruction of what one would commonly find at a park or outdoor event. Some might contain a mailbox or large coffee can within which is placed a roll or two of toilet paper for convenience (although most hikers carry their own) but don't count on running water, hand sanitizer (an item commonly found in thru-hiker backpacks already) or even lighting (window or otherwise).

Passing by a campground in Tennessee, I decided to make use of the privy. Atop a small flight of steps, on a simple wooden platform, sat a fiberglass toilet. All around were trees separated by small fields of grass, and a blue sky above. I felt exposed and vulnerable. A few hours later, I met a hiker anxious to tell me about a bear siting he had that morning. He was sitting on a toilet, atop a small flight of steps, on a simple wooden platform, admiring the grassy fields separating the trees. About 50 feet from his perch, a small bear walks across one of the fields, taking no interest in him. With his pants at his ankles, and no walls to protect him, he was glad the encounter went smoothly. Better him than me.

In Vermont I found several privies that were large enough to comfortably sleep several tired hikers - if you didn't mind the location - and looking very freshly constructed. Later I learned that these privies were oversized because the money used to build them came from the state and that by law they had to be handicapped accessible - never mind the fact that they were miles from any road and accessible only by muddy, root-filled, mountain trails.

And yet there are ways around this law that you'll find in the south. In Tennessee and North Carolina many privies simply consist of a hole in the ground, a wooden floor built on top of it and a plastic/fiberglass toilet placed on top. No walls, no roof, no protection whatsoever. By neglecting to use an actual structure you can subsequently avoid making it handicapped accessible even if the money came from federal funds.

While one could probably plan their hike in such a way as to always find a privy or public bathroom (such as those found in parks or towns), the reality is that sometimes nature calls at unexpected moments and there are no regulations stating you must use a real toilet. For my part, I carried a plastic camp trowel (fancy word for shovel) and it did get a fair bit of use. Best practices may vary, but here are the guidelines I tried to follow for solid waste:

1. Find a location not visible from the trail and at least 200 feet from a water source
2. Gently scrape away the loose top layer of leaves and sticks
3. More purposefully scrape to the side the second layer of the forest floor that usually consists of dark colored earth and debris, representing a type of composted material
4. Dig a hole 6-8 inches deep, setting the dirt carefully aside
5. Do my business and fill back in the hole with dirt. Atop the dirt I attempt to replace the composted layer and atop that I return the loose ground cover
6. Apply hand sanitizer

Dispensing with your body's cache of liquid is much simpler. Find a spot 200 feet away from a water source and at a location where you feel comfortably hidden from view, and let loose. One thing to note about urine is that some privies welcome it and some request that you use a tree before you use the toilet, because, in some cases, urine content will hinder the decomposition process and make it much harder to maintain a healthy environment. It all depends on the type of composting privy constructed.

On a side note, the biggest problem related to urination and thru-hiking is that one will become so accustomed to going wherever and whenever you want, adjusting to town life can be difficult. My bladder always behaved, but some hikers expressed difficulties in convincing their bodies to "hold it." Once, late at night while walking with another hiker back from dinner, he simply "had to go" and found a dark corner of someone's property to relieve himself. He felt awful about it but simply saw no better alternative.

What do you eat?

The foods I ate on the AT were diverse and yet somewhat predictable, once you break it down in to three basic components: salt, fat, sweet.

I observed a pattern among thru-hiker diets. While the strong desire for fatty, high calorie foods (ice cream, chocolate milk, pizza, beer) is obvious, something more profound was apparent. In a pendulum fashion, many hikers would go through a period where their food bag leaned heavily towards salty, followed by a period of sweet, then salty and repeat. It was a clear sign of what the body was lacking and the over compensation of feeding that need. For the most part, I started with a fairly diverse diet and never completely succumbed to this effect, and I am optimistic that my diet was healthier as a result.

I think a lot of people have very good intentions when they start out, planning mail drops of healthy foods and supplements or assuming some can be found along the way. I certainly did a lot of research on diet and, at least for the first month, was very careful with my nutrition. In fact, in that first month, the only candy I had in my pack was an occasional Snickers bar that I'd pick up and eat that day (in the Whites where they're sold at every Hut). This was in stark contrast to my final month on the Trail, when grocery store candy aisles found me paying them a visit.

Since I wasn't doing mail drops, I relied on the Trail to provide and after a while your shopping choices become limited. I was often forced to rely entirely on the groceries found in convenience stores. And so, to my chagrin, my diet was far from stellar at times, but as long as my strength and spirit held up, I figured it was OK. Of course, I also had the financial backing that allowed me to eat good, healthy foods while I was in town to help counter my trail diet.

For the first two months I had a fairly consistent menu. I would basically snack all day on:

- Granola bars and yogurt bars, especially in the morning (sugar to help wake me up)
- Clif bars or other energy bars - but I only ate them occasionally and mostly saved them for days when I needed a bigger energy reserve or was out of everything else
- Deluxe salted mixed nuts (no peanuts! It seems peanuts are in everything these days, I didn't need to eat them raw too)
- Beef jerky
- Dried apricots or prunes
- Snyder's flavored pretzel pieces (not the pretzel bites, it has to be the pieces!)
- Pepperoni or sardines on tortilla shells with cheese (the individual serving sized cheddar blocks)
- Apples and oranges
- Carrot sticks

Then for dinner I would cook:

- Lipton pasta sides
- Lipton or similar rice sides
- Flavored instant mashed potatoes
- Mix in some tuna, quinoa (a complete protein grain) or textured vegetable protein (TVP)

I eventually stopped cooking but for a few more weeks carried my stove with a couple ounces of fuel and a Lipton packet or two for emergency purposes. At some point, I decided to put it all in a bounce box for use later. Later, I would send the stove home entirely. I had always enjoyed the relaxation that came with cooking, but it was time for a change. Personal choice aside, there are also several very practical reasons to prepare dinner with ready-to-eat foods.

No more dishes to be done. It's one less thing to do before bed, but it also means a little less water wasted - especially handy during drought conditions. When doing dishes, I always did a first rinse and scrub without soap, drank the "gray water," and then finished with a soapy rinse that got dispersed in the woods.

Less weight? I'm still not sure if stove or stoveless is lighter. On the one hand, you're not carrying a stove, pot or fuel. On the other hand, ready-to-eat foods tend to weigh a lot more than dehydrated. Then again, as with the dishes argument, during a drought I rather liked having the high moisture content in my food already, even if I did have to carry it.

Drought. I liked the security of knowing that at the end of the day I would have dinner no matter how bad the drought was. With water in short supply, there was a good chance I could finish the day without (or with just barely) enough to cook dinner. Plus, I like to go to bed with enough water to get me to the next source in the morning, or even until the afternoon.

On the other hand, it was sometimes hard or even impossible to find the appropriate foods to serve for dinner, especially when shopping at convenience stores. A typical pre-cooked dinner would include wraps or tortillas stuffed with any or all of the following:

- Cream cheese! Yummy cream cheese!!!
- Cooked tuna, salmon, crab and chicken in single serving packages or cans
- Slices of cheese or preferably an individual cheese stick or two
- Mayonnaise and/or mustard and/or ketchup and/or Arby's Horsey Sauce
- If I was lucky, I would also add bell pepper and/or pre-cooked bacon

- Occasionally I'd go straight for the good stuff and wrap a tortilla shell around a 4 oz bar of cream cheese (I didn't realize they made them that small!)

For the last two months of hiking, I added a few things to my snacking list:

- Combos or Pringles - I grew tired of Snyder's pretzels
- Target brand, all natural fruit bars
- Breakfast danishes (preferably Lance brand)
- Lance brand cheesy crackers (seriously, after trying half a dozen brands, Lance stood out as having THE BEST quality and flavor in every snack category)
- Fig Newton's, Oreos, Vienna Fingers or Nutter Butters

I would be remiss if I didn't mention the sub shops and delis. A particular luxury was carrying a sub or sandwich from town to eat as dinner - or buy an extra one for lunch. Just be sure to order it without tomatoes or condiments if you need to save it for a while lest it get soggy. I even had a few occasions to carry leftover pizza still in the box.

It's time to talk more about candy. From Maine to New York the only "sugar" I carried was a Snickers bar usually eaten right after purchase. I was simply turned off by the idea of carrying something that served so little nutritional value. I figured if I wanted the protein and fat of a Snickers bar, I'd just eat raw nuts instead.

Then, just before New Jersey I met up with and hiked for 350 miles with Lady and her dog, Tramp. Lady always had Swedish Fish or Sour Patch Kids candy and she got me hooked. It's almost shameful that from that point on I would frequently have either of those candies in my pack. It became something to look forward to - if I do 28 miles today I can have some Swedish Fish with my dinner!

Then, in Shenandoah National Park, Virginia, I met a nice family that absolutely insisted I take their package of Vienna Fingers cookies. We compromised and I took half. At that point a cookie light bulb turned on in my head and I rarely went without Vienna Fingers, Oreos or Nutter Butters from that point on.

How did you take care of your trash?

I had a system where I always had a sealable container available to carry my trash safely. Whatever you choose for yourself, it should be something that won't open easily, will contain the dry, wet, or smelly contents appropriately, and is fairly compact. It could be an empty just-add-water meal container, a zippable baggy, a Pringles container, or a grocery bag that can be tied.

I would often find garbage cans while walking through town, parking lots, trailheads, or parks. Sometimes day-hikers or locals I'd meet would offer to dispose of it for me.

Generally speaking, you should not burn your trash to dispose of it. You could cause a forest fire and/or inhale toxic chemicals put off by the materials in the packaging. Even after being burned, some food smells may still linger and attract animals - not to mention it's an eyesore to anyone coming upon a pile of ash in an otherwise peaceful outdoor environment.

What did you do with your food at night?

What did I do with my food at night? I ate it, of course! Oh, you mean how did I store it for the night OUTSIDE of my stomach?

The basic idea is that you want the food, or any objects with an odor, stored away from where you are camping and out of reach of animals. Even if something isn't edible, or you can't smell it, or it has a foul odor, it doesn't mean it's safe to keep it with you for the night. Toothpaste, toothbrush, ChapStick, ointments, drink mixes in sealed packages, and so on can and will attract animals.

One reason this is important to note is that mice, rats or any rodent might have learned that while the bristles of your toothbrush are yucky, perhaps the handle has some salt on it from your hand and they're more than happy to chew the plastic to get at it. Anyone ever had a dog that chewed a tube of ChapStick just to eat the flavored waxy substance inside? I knew a dog that enjoyed eating scented plastic balls for deodorizing shoes!

Another reason is one of association. Bears, in particular, are known for learning that where there's toothpaste there's probably something else worth rooting around for. Trust me, you'd much rather have a bear trying to get at your food bag than have it come into your tent or lean-to because it was feeling peckish. In New Mexico, a ranger once told me that even batteries should go in the food bag at night. I'm still not sold on that one.

All my smellables would go in to what is called a "bear bag" but it can be any container that you can tie one end of a rope or cord to. In my case it was a nylon stuff sack that was breathable and not terribly water resistant (so that it would breathe and keep the contents a little cooler) that I picked up for probably a couple dollars at an outfitter along with 50 feet of parachute cord.

Once you have your bear bag situated, you need to get it off the ground, and placed so that animals have a hard time getting to it. Many shelters will have things that look like very tall coat racks stuck in the ground that you can hang your bags on by using a long pole with a hook. Many shelters have large metal storage boxes with latches that bears haven't figured out how to open. In the Smoky Mountains, the shelters have very neat looking cable and pulley systems for hanging large numbers of bags.

If you have to fend for yourself, it's best to find a tree branch that's well suited to throwing a rope over and will support the weight of your bag. The branch should be high enough off the ground so that bears can't reach it, thin enough that a bear can't walk out on it, long enough that a bear can't climb up the trunk and reach over to grab your bag and with no nearby branches that would give the bear access to your branch.

After finding a location that meets these criteria, you have to decide what method to use for hanging your food. It's no longer recommended to do the quick and dirty "tie one end to a tree" method, since bears have learned to look for this and cut through the rope, letting the bag fall to the ground. However, I did use this method sparingly in places where bears were not known to be or if there weren't any good tree branch options – places where even a turtle could probably get to it.

For the most part I used the Pacific Crest Trail method (or PCT method) since it does not involve tying one end to anything at all. The

PCT method starts by tying a rock to one end of the rope and throwing it over the branch. The other end is tied to your bag along with a tiny key chain style carabiner. Remove the rock and pass that end of the rope through the carabiner. Find a sturdy twig on the ground and hold onto it. You can now hoist your bag in the air, all the way up to the branch. While holding on to the rope, reach as high as you can and tie the twig to the rope. Let go of the rope slowly and let the bag slide back down to the ground, watching it stop as the twig tries to pass through the carabiner. Hopefully your bag is still at least 10 feet off the ground and away from even the tallest bear.

To retrieve your bag, simply grab the loose end of the rope and pull it until you can reach the twig, set it free, and then lower the bag.

The only problem I found with this method is that if your rope is thin, and your carabiner is too close to the end secured to your bag, the twig might get caught in the bag and not want to come back down when you pull on the rope. To get around this, I was fortunate to have a four inch long handle on my food bag. On one end of the handle I could tie the rope and on the other end could be the carabiner. This separation was enough to prevent the twig from binding up amongst the bag, cord and carabiner.

More thoughts on stinking up camp

While you may be tempted to cook and/or eat your dinner comfortably tucked inside your warm tent or shelter, it is not the best idea. The lingering smells may attract curious animals. Some people would recommend eating dinner while you are still hiking so that dinner and camping are separated by a good distance. Another recommendation is to prepare and eat dinner away from your shelter, especially if the lean-to area provides a picnic table.

While it's best to observe these practices, the reality is that you won't find many people doing this on the AT. Nor is it as important here as it is on trails out West – especially when grizzlies become a factor.

On the AT, people will lay out all their food in the lean-to, prepare dinner, spill soup or drop mashed potatoes on the floor, and sleep soundly through the night with nothing to worry about except for the scampering of fat mice.

Even brushing your teeth or doing your dishes should be done away from where you are sleeping. Purists will tell you that you should swallow your toothpaste, but for health reasons I'm not comfortable doing this for weeks at a time. Out West you might have gray water sump pits with screens over them that you can use, but this is rare. This might be a bit vulgar to discuss openly, but my method for toothpaste waste was to spit on the ground away from camp, rinse with fresh water and spit that out on the toothpaste to soak it in to the ground. That's not the vulgar part. I would then urinate in that same spot, to further soak it in to the ground and mask the scent with the generally-offensive-to-animals smell of human urine.

What about food cravings?

For most hikers, a list of their food cravings will most likely involve beer and ice cream. I've never even tolerated the taste of beer, and as for ice cream, I'd have to vote for its close cousin, chocolate milk. I became quite the connoisseur of that brown elixir, and when I couldn't find a brand I liked, I would go for plain ol' fully fat whole milk.

Cravings are partly driven by comfort factor, but necessity is the one truly behind the wheel. You've burned a lot of fat, possibly even muscle, and so the high fat, high carbohydrate foods are usually on top of the list. I didn't particularly crave fruits or vegetables, but for nutrition's sake I tried to gorge on them in towns – although I did have an almost insatiable appetite for melons of all types. Keep in mind that I was one of the very few thru-hikers who habitually carried at least some fresh fruit and vegetables - at least in the second half of the hike when I could better justify the weight.

What I still can't understand is why, for almost 1,800 miles, did I forever hunger for hot dogs? Maybe it was the salt, but I can think of plenty of saltier foods that seem more logical. And why, despite my apparent desire for pizza, did I almost never act on it while I was in town? In practice, while

I was on the Trail, I didn't give much thought to BBQ, but when I hit towns I always hoped to find a BBQ place or at least a pulled-pork sandwich.

When kitchens became available to Southbounders, in the second half of the Trail, I began to salivate over the thought of making my Buffalo chicken dip.

In a glass baking dish, combine:
- 8oz cream cheese
- 8oz sour cream
- 1/4 cup chunky bleu cheese dressing (or to taste)
- 1 1/2 lbs cooked chicken breast (boiled, chilled then shredded)
- 1 cup chopped, sautéed celery (optional)
- Pete's or Frank's Red Hot (or Buffalo) hot sauce to taste
- Place in a 350°F oven until melted, serve with tortilla chips and a side of extra sauce

Health... weight loss?

I'm fortunate to have a healthy constitution and strong immune system – so health wasn't much of a concern for me. But I can't take credit alone for this, since health is largely a factor of diet, which is largely a factor of budget. A lot of hikers complain of being tired or sick all the time and while there are exceptions, many simply aren't eating well. The Ramen Noodles diet, while affordable and appealing to the college student, doesn't contain much nutrition.

Don't skimp on your food budget; I feel it's the most important factor contributing to the success of your hike!

No matter how much money I threw at my stomach, I still lost a significant amount of weight - considering that I wasn't overweight to begin with - but the important thing to consider is that I maintained a healthy disposition, didn't get sick or run-down, and always had a normal energy level.

To compensate for the inevitable weight loss, a few months before my hike, I intentionally ate my way from 170 pounds to 180 pounds and then lost this weight in the first two weeks on the AT. By the end of my first month I hit the scales at 160 pounds, an overall loss of 20 pounds. At the half way mark I weighed 155 pounds and one friend said I looked "svelte" (a compliment) while another said I looked "really skinny" (not a compliment). While I was flattered to be called svelte, I was concerned that my six foot tall frame did, in fact, look quite skinny. However, I took solace in the fact that my weight loss had slowed down significantly and my weight seemed to be holding steady.

Fat deposits in my mid-section were the first to go and while I still had most of my body muscle, there was no longer a thin layer of fat protecting them. I basically looked like a marathon runner - which is not exactly a desirable physique for a backpacker.

When my body weight hit 155 pounds, I realized that I was dangerously close to burning off muscle mass, now that the fat was gone, so I did my best to put back on the pounds and eat more while hiking. By the time I reached Georgia, my weight was still around 155 pounds but I managed to put back on a thin layer of fat around each muscle, giving me a more healthy appearance.

How did my weight stay the same while apparently gaining fat? It turns out I lost the muscle in my legs that I had from bicycling, which was not needed for hiking and replaced it with general body mass.

With such a healthy and voracious appetite, it should come as no surprise that in only a few months after the Trail, I was right back up to my body's natural weight of 170 pounds.

Want to hear some other numbers? I met an ex-thru-hiker that lost 70 pounds and put 80 pounds back on. A fellow I briefly hiked with had lost 40 pounds. They say women tend not to lose as much weight as men, and this seemed to hold true based on the women I met on and off the trail.

Did you use sun screen?

No ma'am, I did not even carry sun screen. But then again my Caucasian complexion isn't exactly fair.

The AT is very much a green tunnel with relatively little exposure to the rays of the sun - but of course there are exceptions. Starting on Mount Katahdin, you're exposed to a lot of direct sun light for a lengthy period of time - Adam and I did get a mild sunburn there. In New Hampshire you are above tree line for a significant amount of time - though I was more likely to be burned by the low clouds.

The long treeless ridges of New Jersey, New York and Pennsylvania also have a good bit of exposure, but by the time a thru-hiker gets here we have already developed a sufficiently protective tan that getting a burn isn't as likely.

By the time I got to the bald mountains in the south, the summer sun had long-since passed and the cooler temperatures often found me in long sleeves anyway.

Spending all that time outside, with the canopy coming and going, you're going to slowly build up a good base rather than go directly to a burn. If you take Katahdin out of the equation, I think a thru-hiker starting at either end of the AT will have it pretty good. Of course, there are exceptions and I'm sure those who burn easily should consider carrying sun screen, at least until you've had enough experience to know just how much solar exposure you can handle.

Do you carry water or do you make it?

In the lobby of Amicalola Lodge after I had completed the AT, I had a conversation about my experiences with two older couples clearly not from outdoor upbringings. One lady asked me, "Do you carry water or do you make it?" I didn't understand the question; I wasn't quite sure how one could make water. So I prompted her to clarify, "Are you asking if I buy water from a store or if I filter or treat water from streams?" "No," she replied, "Do you make it?" I looked at her husband for help and, looking equally perplexed, he changed the subject.

Whatever she meant, the topic of water is certainly a good one. As with many aspects of my gear, I experimented with different ways of handling my water. Southbounders generally start off with an abundance of beautiful looking springs to choose from and have the luxury of ignoring streams and rivers. As time goes by, the springs disappear and you're forced to deal with moving water, the occasional pond and possibly muddy puddles.

At the height of the drought, a section-hiker I met was planning on getting water from a particular spring. When he found it was dry, he was forced to wander downhill to look for another source. Eventually he found a pond... muddy... with cows in it... and floating cow "business." Out of desperation, he was forced to draw water with his pump filter and hope for the best. I can only hope his description of the pond was exaggerated, but even with a pump that water could still be pretty awful tasting.

I started the trip with both Polar Pure iodine as well as a Katadyn (pronounced CAT-uh-dine) pump filter that I would alternate between. After the 100 Mile Wilderness, I sent the pump home with Adam because I didn't want to deal with the inevitable clog or failure - not to mention the financial benefit of using a single, small, $12 bottle of iodine that will serve for the whole AT (and then some).

One of the most popular methods on the AT is Aqua Mira, a system where two chemicals are combined to form a chlorine gas capable of killing bacteria and what-have-you. After a month I was carrying both Polar Pure and Aqua Mira to see which one I'd prefer. To me, both had aftertastes, and both had the drawback that you couldn't drink them right away. The Aqua Mira was more expensive in the long run (but not terribly so), but iodine has a way of killing both the bad AND good microbes in your digestive system - as a result you are urged to eat yogurt whenever you can.

But don't worry too much, iodine has been used by the military, Boy Scouts, and hikers for many years, so its safety is reasonably well researched.

Apparently only a small portion of the population can taste Aqua Mira, and I'm one of them. It has a slightly bitter, chemically citrus-like taste that does tend to subside if you leave the lid off of your water bottle for the gas to dissipate. Iodine tastes like... well... iodine, but with a little vitamin C added to the water, the iodine taste and color disappear completely (to me at least).

In the end, I opted to carry just the Aqua Mira because it didn't discolor my water bottles and the taste was a little better than iodine – often leaving the cap off my water bottle overnight so the chlorine gas could escape.

There were two other popular methods: UV light pens and common sense. You can read about the UV light options somewhere else, but suffice it to say they're becoming quite popular and are known to work just as well as other options. Unfortunately, the only ones on the market require wide mouthed water bottles and would not work with my Platypus hydration set up, so I didn't feel the need to experiment with it.

The common sense method is basically that water sources on the AT (and in most of the country) are far better than we think. The Trail is full of people who walk all 2,200 miles without treating their water and never get sick. The Trail is also full of people that treat every drop as if it were highly volatile and STILL get sick. One reason could be that they treat the water but leave untreated water on the threaded lip of the bottle and end up consuming it the next time they take a drink.

There's also a popular theory that getting an intestinal illness isn't so much a factor of what you drink, as whose hand you're shaking or food you're sharing. Seriously, as we're hiking, we blow our noses into the air then wipe them with our sleeves or hands. We don't exactly wash after every "urination event" - although hopefully we rinse, wash or sanitize our hands after a "bowel event." We might have just splashed water on our face from a contaminated water source. We might have just shaken hands with the dirtiest hiker on the East Coast!

I urge you to set a good example when you share your trail mix, chips or whatever, and pour the food into the person's hands without making contact. I always cringe when I see a hiker (or even a co-worker now) dive in with their hand to grab some communal food. Heebee-jeebees! Going to one extreme, there are hikers who will only carry food they can eat directly from a package in order to avoid even the chance of their own hands contaminating their own food. My approach was to think about what I'd been in contact with before having a meal or snack, and if I did anything "risky," I would wash/rinse/sanitize my hands first.

Certainly buying water, as the lady at Amicalola Lodge may have been suggesting, is not all that feasible for a four to six month hike - the cost alone would ruin you. But I am still surprised how many times I found myself filling up from bathroom sinks and household spigots. For all 40 miles of

Maryland, I never once had to use a natural water source since there were public restrooms, beverage machines and even a hostel to stop at for water. For days at a time in Pennsylvania, I would rely on public water sources, simply because the drought had provided little other choice.

I am far less picky about my water now that I'm back in society and would much rather fill up a water bottle in a gas station sink than spend $1.50 for a bottle of it.

Did you just buy Tang?

I crave calories, I dream of ways to consume more of them, and I'm tired of drinking plain old water - and perhaps a little tired of that Aqua Mira flavor. It shouldn't come as a surprise that a lot of hikers carry some form of drink mix. I had no idea there were so many on the market!

You can walk down the drink aisle and contemplate Kool-Aid, iced tea, Crystal Light, lemonade, Gatorade, PowerAde, and so on. Some use real sugar, some are artificial, and some use a natural sweetener extracted from plants. You'd think flavor and calories (sugar) would be the only factors, until you look at the label on Tang.

Tang doesn't use an artificial sweetener, that's great, but even more interesting to learn is that it actually has a good dose of vitamins and minerals. Yes, orange juice or fresh fruit is better for you, but both can spoil and are hard to carry long distances and Tang certainly seems better than the other options! Oh, and did I mention that it comes in two flavors these days?

I would mix up some Tang in my little water bottle when I needed an extra boost of energy during the day. More often, I would mix some up to have with dinner. I didn't always carry a heavy container of Tang, nor did I always have a form of drink mix, but more often than not I tried to have one or two individual serving size packets of a drink mix in case I needed it (for energy or to hide the taste of bad water).

Do you ever shower? Laundry?

You can obviously shower when you get to a town, which for me was anywhere from one to six days away. When the weather was cooler and sweating wasn't an issue, I would sometimes pass up the chance for a shower if it had only been a few days.

In Maryland, there's a public bathroom facility on the Trail with free showers and in other states you might find yourself in parks or campgrounds with running water. Some shelters even had spring fed solar-showers - although the water temperature would suggest our sun is dying - and a good number had showers fed by public water systems. It's worth noting that Northbounders will find hot water at most (all?) of the public water facilities, but that in my case the hot water had been shut off because either it was "out of season" or there was a "possibility of freezing temperatures" (as signs would apologetically state).

On several occasions I'd hear the comment, "Funny, you don't smell like a thru-hiker" even though I tend to sweat like a glass of ice water on a hot day. I think I gained this reputation because, early on, I began doing three things that helped with this common hygiene issue:

First, every night I would take a bandana bath (think "sponge bath"). Depending on availability, this could involve as little as 2/3 cup of water. Furthermore, when it rained, I would not change into rain gear, opting simply to have the precipitation cleanse my clothing and backpack straps. Even when it grew bitterly cold, I didn't wear rain gear in a storm - although at times I wish I had. The problem with rain gear is that unless it's really cold, you're just going to sweat in it and end up drenched, so you might as well just let Mother Nature do the work for you. I'm sure I surprised those weekend hikers in Shenandoah National Park when I stood, fully clothed, in the rain, under a broken gutter hanging from a lean-to roof. Sure I was then covered in dead bugs and debris, but I didn't smell any more!

Second, I had "clean" clothes that I would put on after I took a bandana bath. This could be my town clothes, long underwear or simply a pair of boxers dedicated to sleeping in. Generally, the bath was the last thing I'd do before hopping into bed.

Third, I used a silk sleeping bag liner that kept my sleeping bag from acquiring a funky smell that could then make me smell worse. Down sleeping bags are difficult to wash/dry because they require special soap and a very long, low temperature drying time. Conversely, synthetic sleeping bags are more forgiving and easy to wash almost anywhere. If I were to go the synthetic route I might not have cared so much about clean sleep clothes.

In order to save some money, laundry was not something I did in every town, but it was generally done on a weekly basis. Motels and hostels often had laundry facilities (some free, some coin operated) and sometimes you'd need to find a Laundromat. In one motel, the owner complained that thru-hikers destroy laundry machines by overloading and abusing them, so he insisted on doing my laundry for me, for free.

23. A Walk in Virginia

Looking at the iconic McAfee Knob with Virginia in the background.

Length:	550 miles	885 km
Max Elevation:	5,500 feet	1,676 m
Min Elevation:	265 feet	81 m
My First Day:	September 5	
My Last Day:	October 8	

What's it like?

Virginia is the longest state on the Appalachian Trail and is one of those states hikers can't wait to put behind them, simply because it's such a big achievement.

Having officially left the north (you see a sign for the Mason-Dixon Line in southern Pennsylvania), you will find that it still takes a while before you really meet the south. Northern Virginia is so close to major cities that, although you do start seeing "Sweet Tea" and "Biscuits and Gravy" on the menus, you can't yet hear the southern accent on the lips of locals.

The Trail does its best to skirt the western side of the state, often within reach of West Virginia. From a preservation perspective, this part of the state has done well for itself. There are numerous national forests and parks and rarely do you find yourself outside of one of their protective borders.

Virginia is also home to many great, often historic, hostels and Trail towns. You may have heard of Damascus, Virginia, home to the biggest thru-hiker gathering on the Trail - a weekend long celebration called Trail Days. There's Bears Den Hostel, an old fieldstone mansion converted into a hostel with all the comforts of home and a small supply of microwave meals, drinks and snacks. When I hiked the AT, there was a great hostel on church grounds atop a hill overlooking Pearisburg, Virginia, just a short walk through a field to a WalMart with groceries – but I believe it was recently closed due to ongoing problems with vandalism and theft. Maybe it will re-open.

The diversity of wildlife and landscape makes Virginia a truly wonderful state. I saw a dozen bears, walked through cow pastures, passed through packs of wild ponies, saw foxes, turtles, rattlesnakes and black rat snakes. You

A mansion converted in to a beautiful hostel. The Bears Den is one of those must-stay places.

will cross over rivers, walk along exposed rock and forested ridges, climb to the tops of mountains, walk through large fields, find yourself admiring the vast wildflower meadows (or in my case, grass and scrub), smell wild onions baking in the sun, and stroll down Main Street looking for the Laundromat.

You will eventually transition to yet another ridge of the Appalachians near Roanoke, Virginia, and at one point you see a sign marking the Eastern Continental Divide. Rain landing on one side of the sign contributes to the Gulf of Mexico watershed, while the other goes to the Atlantic.

1,920 miles to the Gulf doesn't seem like a lot when you've walked here from Maine.

I'm not sure if it was my timing, or the culture, but it was in the southern part of the state that I began running in to people carrying rifles on the Trail. Many claimed they were hunting squirrel or in some places deer, and I was glad to be wearing a bright orange tee-shirt (it wasn't intentional; it was just the cheapest synthetic shirt I found on a store clearance rack). I don't recall, however, ever hearing a gun shot in these days.

A few highlights

Shenandoah National Park is a phenomenal park to visit whether you're looking to drive the ridge top Skyline Drive and see the views from inside your car, take a hike on the Appalachian Trail or walk on any of the numerous side trails. Parking lots, overviews and rest stops are numerous in the park and nearly every one will service a trail of some kind. As an AT thru-hiker, I find it appealing that you can travel light and rely on rest stops (or waysides) for food and supplies throughout Shenandoah. At just over 100 miles in length, the trail through the park isn't something you'll do in a weekend, but because you can travel light and can find rangers, tourists, and park facilities quite easily, it's a fairly safe way to try long-distance hiking and backpacking. Personally, I prefer the southern half of the park because it's relatively isolated (most tourists stay in the more developed northern half). Although, with so many great views, side trails to waterfalls and shelters, you can't go wrong in any part of the park.

Leaving the southern end of Shenandoah, you'll perform a quick hop across a gap in the mountain range where a highway has found a home. You'll suddenly end up on the Blue Ridge Parkway (BRP), inside the George Washington National Forest. Extending 460 miles from the Smoky Mountains in North Carolina to Shenandoah, the BRP is amazingly popular and well traveled. Unlike Shenandoah, there is no paid entry, and just like Shenandoah there are park facilities, rest stops, overviews and plenty of hiking. The AT heads in roughly the same direction as the BRP for about 100 miles before branching off just north of Roanoke to head over to the Jefferson National Forest, never to return. The Trail along the Blue Ridge Parkway is undeveloped and gorgeous. Re-supplying might not be the easiest (requiring a hitchhike or long walks on narrow twisting roads), but drivers in this part of the country are used to picking up people with backpacks.

I would be remiss if I didn't mention one of the most visited sections of the AT: McAfee Knob. McAfee Knob is an easy day hike from a major parking lot on a major road outside of Roanoke, Virginia. You will frequently find buses and vans unloading their passengers, and because there is an alternate route along a fire road, you'll find people of all shapes, sizes and conditions making the journey. If you go in the middle of the week, or get there early on a weekend, it's not quite so populated, but even if you do go at the height of fall foliage on a gorgeous Saturday, the view is worth it. McAfee Knob is a large slab of rock jutting a dozen feet out from the top of a cliff, with nothing underneath to support it. It offers you about a 270 degree view of the Jefferson National Forest and includes a multitude of Appalachian ridges going off as far as the eye can see. Just be aware that there is no camping near the Knob, but there are two shelters between it and the parking lot.

Always a fan of the underdog, I actually prefer Tinker Cliffs to McAfee Knob. The cliffs are several miles away from McAfee and aren't as picturesque, but I think they afford an equal view with far fewer people and even the option of camping just feet from the edge. You can get to Tinker Cliffs either by the same parking lot you'd use for McAfee or from the opposite direction by way of the AT from Daleville or by a much closer parking lot and side trail at the base of the mountain.

Walking through Grayson Highlands State Park is one of the most interesting experiences for anyone hiking part, or all, of the AT. Located a few miles from the North Carolina border, and almost at the end of the Trail in Virginia, this park is comprised of forest, bald mountain tops and vast meadows strewn with large boulders. It's unlike anything a Southbounder has seen and marks the start of "the balds," referring to mountains that are incapable of growing anything but grasses on their summit. But what really makes Grayson stand out are the packs of wild ponies roaming free (albeit within its fenced borders). These are the same ponies that you find on the Assateague and Chincoteague Islands off of the Maryland and Virginia coasts. The hiking itself is worth the visit, but adding ponies makes it even more special.

24. Gear

How many shoes have you gone through?

One of the funnier statistics about the AT is related to footwear. Taking five million steps on mostly uneven, often rocky, terrain can take its toll and the footwear you choose will determine how often you have to buy replacements.

Generally speaking, full-leather traditional hiking boots will hold up the best, but you should still plan on buying one replacement pair. Lightweight hiking shoes will last 500-800 miles (three to four pairs). Sneakers will last 400-600 miles (four to six pairs).

The numbers aren't perfect, but are still a pretty good approximation one should consider when making a budget. Ultimately, it all depends on how heavy you and your pack are, how gently you tread, how careful you are about taking care of them, what brand/quality you've bought, and how lucky you are.

Personally, I think I'm part Leprechaun because, of the five pairs of footwear I used on the AT, three of them I still wear often (they're still in near-perfect shape), one did fall apart, and the other I outgrew quickly. If I had my crystal ball and knew what size I needed, what the weather would be like, and what style was best for me, I'm certain I could have made it with only one pair of trail runners and one pair of hiking sandals.

How did you carry water?

Hikers tend to fall in to one of three categories: Platypus, Camelback, or other. The first two are hydration bags that use hoses and valves to access the water, while "other" involves everything else.

I always carried a small Nalgene water bottle with a very wide mouth - durable and great for dipping into water sources or making drink mixes. Next up was a two to three liter Platypus (or several depending on the drought) that I would either fill directly from the water source or use my Nalgene as an intermediary. In the 100 Mile Wilderness, I would drink from my Nalgene as I hiked, stopping to refill it from my Platypus. I then experimented with the hose attachment and never went back simply because of its convenience. I would store the Platypus inside my backpack and snake the hose to the chest strap for easy access.

The Camelback behaves much the same way - except for some key differences. The Platypus is collapsible yet is made out of a stiffer plastic that allows it to stand up, while the Camelback just sort of flops around like a wet noodle. This trait of the Platypus also allows it to be filled up easier in shallow water sources (think of what happens when you hold a water bottle under water) while the Camelback needs to be supported off the ground to allow it to expand freely (try filling a Ziploc baggy with water without holding it). It's easier to find replacement parts for Camelbacks and because of their wide mouth you just might be able to use a UV light treatment pen.

The one thing I would recommend when hiking in warm weather is that you choose NOT to store your hydration bag in that convenient pocket inside your backpack. You know the one I mean, it's right there up against your back, absorbing all that body heat and turning your cold, refreshing, spring water in to something depressingly tepid. I stored mine on top of my pack (accessible and not TOO bad for proper weight distribution) and occasionally stored an extra one in that pocket when I needed to carry more.

As far as other options are concerned, the sky is the limit. Used, small soda bottles were common and I'd even see the occasional hose sticking out of one to mimic a hydration bag. The larger Nalgenes, although heavy, were quite common, as were all the knock-off brands. As long as you have a water bottle pocket or two on the side of your backpack within easy reach, this is not an unreasonable way to go, you just might have to stop more often to refill them.

No matter what solution you choose, remember that if you use your water bottle or bag for a flavored beverage, you may discover one of two things. Either you'll wake up to find your bag/bottle leaking from small holes that developed miraculously during the night (hello rodents!) or your hose will become disgustingly discolored. As such, the only thing I ever put in my Platypus was water.

What's in your pack? Weight?

Without food and water, my pack weighed about 15 pounds during the warm months and 18 pounds with my cold weather clothing - this is called the "base weight." Once I put in five days worth of food and water for one day the scales would tip around 30 pounds. This is generally average for thru-hikers and is considered going lightweight. But I knew people that were in the ultralight category, which is somewhere closer to 15 pounds WITH food and water. One fellow I met was carrying a mere eight pounds without food and water and he would generally carry less water and food than me - but that also meant he would have to stop in towns more often. On the other end of the spectrum were the heavyweights (more than 40 pounds) and the ultra-heavyweights (more than 50 pounds).

Pack weight isn't just about how much food and water you carry, it's primarily about the type and amount of gear. For financial reasons, many people will choose to carry a four pound tent instead of a two pound version. Or a four pound sleeping bag instead of one weighing one and a half pounds. If I had decided to save money and just use all the equipment I'd had since my Boy Scouts days, I could easily have had a base weight of 30 pounds.

But it's not entirely finances making the decision, it's also a comfort factor. There's a tendency to carry something old and heavy, simply because you know it works and would rather not risk experimenting. Not only did I fight this urge, I tried to experiment with all my gear so that I could improve for the next long trail.

I met a man from Virginia carrying 67 pounds (with food and water) who claimed that he had no reason to lighten his load since he'd already made it 1,000 miles. To him, this was proof that he could "obviously make it the remaining 500 miles!" What many people told him, and what he refused to believe, was that until now his hike had been relatively mild and that the remaining 500 miles included the most formidable terrain of the entire Trail, like the White Mountains. At the end of each day, his 60 year old frame could barely move, his joints locked up, his muscles cramped. He was thin as a rail and had lost over 40 pounds. I joined his traveling companions in trying to convince him to lighten his load.

His two-man tent weighed seven pounds, more than double the weight of most hiker's shelters - a lighter tent isn't even that expensive. He had canned food, two extra sets of clothing in case of emergency, two large bottles of fuel when one would easily suffice (most people carried just one small bottle), four extra pairs of AA batteries (when just one set would have done) and so on. He claimed money wasn't a concern for him, so he could have afforded lighter gear, it was mostly that he was just stubborn. True, he'd never in 1,000 miles used any of his extra clothing (perhaps 5 pounds worth), or batteries, or fuel, "but you never know," he'd say.

It's a trade-off between physical comfort and mental comfort. I could live without rain gear because I enjoyed getting wet, while some people would rather go without food than their rain coat.

I did carry some little things that I could have left at home but liked having just in case; like a slightly bigger knife (great size for blocks of cheese and pepperoni though), compass (only ever used the mirror to get debris out of my eyes), first aid supplies (hardly used any of it and could have relied solely on duct tape), and an extra Platypus water bladder in case one sprung a leak.

I could have shaved one pound from my gear if I left behind everything I didn't use on a regular basis, which meant I didn't have many options available if I wanted to go ultralight. I could have shaved a little more than a pound by using a lighter hammock; another five ounces with an expensive sleeping bag and maybe two pounds by investing in more expensive lightweight clothing. I was carrying a backpack that weighed 3.7 pounds and could have gone lighter, but then it might not have held up as well or felt as comfortable. These are all the factors one has to consider when budgeting for gear.

As for the specifics, here's an example of what I was carrying when the weather was cold and the water was relatively scarce:

Pack, Bag and Tent

- Deuter ACT Lite 65+10 packpack
- EMS 30°F down sleeping bag
- Sea To Summit ripstop silk sleeping bag liner
- Hennessy Explorer Asym Hammock without rain fly
- Hennessy SuperShelter
- "Blackeyed Susie" Rain Fly (homemade with a LOT of help from my friend Susie; based on the BlackCat design)

Miscellaneous

- Stuff-sack for groceries
- Stuff-sack containing food for just the day
- Stuff-sack with sleep-related stuff (sleeping bag, silk liner, boxers for warm nights, long johns for cold nights, fleece shirt for a pillow and extra cold nights)
- Stuff-sack with all other clothes
- 2 3-liter Platypus water bottles
- Generic Bic lighter (in case I needed fire)
- Petzl eLite head lamp
- Spare batteries for Petzl lamp
- Canon SD800 IS 28mm digital camera
- Extra camera battery
- Extra 2Gig SD Memory card
- Generic pen and a Sharpie marker for backup
- Compass with mirror
- 50 feet of 550 parachute cord
- Wingfoot data book

Kitchen

- Lexan large spoon
- Fixed-blade knife with 1.5 inch blade
- Aqua Mira water treatment

Clothing

- Long sleeve EMS Techwick shirt

- North Face zip-off pants
- Nylon/spandex ExOfficio boxers
- Fifteen year old Columbia hat
- REI running shorts/swimsuit
- Loose, orange EMS Techwick tee-shirt
- 2 pair socks (one for sleeping in, one for hiking)
- EMS Techwick thermal underwear top
- EMS Techwick thermal underwear bottoms
- Fleece gloves
- Fleece balaclava
- North Face TKA 100 fleece top (primarily as a pillow)

Footwear
- $7 Knock-off Crocs from Target (camp shoes)
- Chaco sandals (for hiking, used both ZX/2 and Z/2 models)

Wallet
- Credit card
- Calling card
- List of phone numbers
- Blood-type card
- Insurance card
- Cash
- ATM card

Essentials
- Bandana
- Hand sanitizer
- Toothbrush (half of the handle cut off)
- Travel tube of toothpaste
- Roll of toilet paper

First aid kit
- Aspirin
- Benadryl (in case of allergic reactions)
- Assorted bandages and gauze
- Imodium AD (just in case, but never used)
- Triple antibiotic ointment

- Safety pins
- Sewing needle
- Dental floss (great for sewing repairs)

What's in your bounce box?

First off: what's a bounce box!? If you're paying attention, you've heard me using the term "bounce" a few times and have probably gathered a relatively accurate definition on your own. A bounce box is a shippable container of some kind that you put various odds and ends in and mail ahead to some town in your future.

This idea works great when you make use of the US Postal Service Priority Mail system. In case you weren't aware, mail sent by Priority Mail can be forwarded as many times as you'd like, without incurring any additional fees - so long as the package has not been opened. I could send a package containing a cell phone charger, extra bug spray, extra clothing, a different sleeping bag, camera batteries or memory cards, and hard to find food from Monson, Maine, to the post office in Gorham, New Hampshire. When I get to Gorham, I can't think of anything I need from the box so I bounce it (for free) ahead to a post office in Manchester, Vermont. When I get to Manchester I still don't need it, so I mail it (for free) to Connecticut. And so on.

If I decide there is something I need, I will take the box from the friendly post office employee, open it up, remove what I want and probably add an item or two. Then I'll have them seal the box and bill me for shipping to the next location. Every post office on the trail provided free packing tape for my Priority Mail parcels, but it's not USPS policy and I've had many post office employees away from the AT angrily tell me to buy packing tape if I need it. Try to use Priority Mail boxes that seal themselves to avoid the packing tape battle.

So, what was in my bounce box? It was generally pretty small and usually pretty pathetic. Initially, it had items like a phone charger, camera batteries and charger, memory cards, extra tent stakes, socks and maps. With so little in my bounce box, I began to realize that making time to visit the post office just to bounce the box ahead was inefficient. That's when I simply carried the phone charger (it weighed almost nothing anyway), my camera accessories were almost never needed, and I didn't really need to keep shipping these blasted tent stakes from town to town Why do I even have extra tent stakes!?

So I pretty much stopped using a bounce box but would occasionally revive the practice when I knew I'd be going through a stretch where the grocery stores were non-existent. I'd put some random staples (like Tang, Pringles and Vienna Fingers) in a bounce box and send them on their way.

In short, I used one in the beginning when I was counting the ounces, then gave up on the practice, unless I needed to worry about food supplies.

What stove do you use?

I had always used the MSR Whisperlite before the Trail (the all-time classic multi-fuel stove) and assumed this is what I'd carry. But then I read a seemingly infinite number of stove debates and decided to experiment.

If you go to an outfitter, chances are you're going to have a large number of choices of traditional, pressurized stove systems like your MSR's, your JetBoil's, and your SnowPeak's. These stoves work by ejecting pressurized fuels through a burner. The problem is that you have to carry a relatively heavy metal fuel canister and a relatively heavy stove.

The alternative is to use a denatured alcohol stove with fuel that can be stored in lightweight plastic bottles and whose burner can be made of lightweight metals like titanium or even old aluminum soda cans. Denatured alcohol is also sold in more places - like drugstores, hardware stores and outfitters - than the white gas or propane needed for pressurized stoves (not that you'll ever have a problem finding either).

Alcohol camp stoves work on the premise that, once a few ounces of liquid alcohol in the stove are ignited, the flames begin to heat up the metal of the stove. The metal heats up to the point where the liquid alcohol begins to boil. The gas created ignites and steals the oxygen from the liquid, thereby creating its own pressurized gas burner. I find it a fascinating concept.

The primary problem with alcohol stoves is that it's harder to heat the metal and create the gas in cold temperatures. Often this means you have to pour extra fuel into the burner or pour some around the outside of the stove to prime it properly. At a certain point it can become too cold for the stove to work at all. Unless you're hiking in the dead of winter, you probably won't have this problem on the AT.

In the months prior to my start, I became what they call a "stove addict." I was bound and determined to design and build the perfect alcohol stove, using ideas from dozens of different homemade designs available on the internet. During my first month on the AT, I alternated among two homemade designs and two store-bought. Because of their low weight, I could easily carry two at a time.

Pepsi can stove

Made from two used soda cans, the Pepsi can stove is very popular. I found it to be VERY light, very easy, and very cost-effective. I also found that it put off too large a flame for my pot, and therefore less efficient. It is basically the bottoms from two soda cans, sandwiched together.

Cat food can stove

The cat food can stove is popular because of how easy it is to build. You just need a hole punch and an old can (preferably the small size) of cat food. It worked very well, but it put out too much flame for my liking. It also seemed the least safe to use.

Trangia Mini

This brass stove was purchased online and I am forever impressed with the quality of construction. Even though it was by far the heaviest, I found this to be my stove of choice for a few reasons. The flame was somewhat adjustable, the stove itself was also a modest fuel storage container, and it gave off a smaller flame better suited to my pot.

Vargo Triad

The Vargo Triad was my only Titanium stove. I really liked this stove, but my specific model requires a lot of fuel just to get to the point where you can prime it, which means I was wasting fuel. In theory, you can blow it out and pour the excess fuel back in to your bottle, but that was messy. Newer Vargo models look like big improvements and are worth  trying. Once again, however, the flame was too much for me.

And then there's the "no stove" option. Your food might be heavier since it won't be dehydrated, but you won't have to carry heavy fuel so it seems like it balances out. I found it a logical choice too, considering that the drought meant I might not have enough water to cook dinner. I was also happy to have a menu change.

Gear advice - how to buy?

I've become a gear snob. I find myself in my local outfitters, offering advice and giving direction to customers when the staff isn't around. One of these days I'm sure I'll be blacklisted from these stores. Some hikers go from Maine to Georgia with the same stuff on their back and body, but I'd been fortunate in that I was able to experiment with different brands and styles of gear.

I'm really struggling here. I want to bad-mouth the brands that failed me (often on more than one occasion with more than one product) and I want to lavish my respect all over the manufacturers that did me well. The problem is that I also want to remain impartial and somewhat timeless - since what might be a miserably failing backpack company one year, might turn around the next year with a great new product.

Let me explain gear buying with an example. The final item I needed for my hike was a backpack and I found myself in Washington, DC, with enough time to hit up two different outfitters. Each one raved about the pack I eventually bought, claiming they sell a lot of them to thru-hikers and not one has ever been returned. Sounds great! I'll take it! This pack didn't last more than five days before it suffered severe failure in the hip and shoulder straps. I heard from several outfitters located on the Trail that the pack, and even that brand, is far from reliable. One outfitter decided not to carry the brand because all he ever did was returns and exchanges for them.

Was I lied to in DC? Not really. You see, those DC stores probably never did have that pack returned by a thru-hiker, because all those returns take place directly with the manufacturer or in an outfitter on the Trail. After all, I'm not about to fly from Maine to DC just to return a pack!

The gentleman I met in Maine who started off with five knives, fell victim to exactly this. An outfitter in Texas had no experience with true camping or backpacking and sold him everything they possibly could. He started the AT carrying a 54 pound backpack and at least 20 pounds of that was excess. Remember, just because it's in the camping section doesn't mean it's for backpackers.

What can you do to avoid problems like this? If at all possible, find an outfitter located on or near a major trail system that really knows what they're talking about. Regardless of the quality of your outfitter, it's important that you try on or examine several alternatives, even if you don't think you'll like them. That line of shoes might look horribly ugly and uncomfortable compared to another, but it might fit your feet perfectly and cosmetics really don't matter. That jacket might be really ugly, but guess what, it weighs four ounces and costs $40 while that "normal" looking jacket weighs two pounds and costs $200. Don't limit yourself only to aesthetics and popular opinion.

And remember the mantra "DON'T BUY IT!" Just because that jacket is light and cheap, and those shoes are flawlessly comfortable, doesn't mean you should buy it. Go home, think about it and most importantly do some research! Maybe that flashlight can't handle a drop from more than two feet, or the pants are notoriously easy to rip. There are clothes treated with bug repellent, advertised as a great way to fend off the mosquitoes. Sounds wonderful until you read reviews that suggest sweat can neutralize the effect of the chemical (you'll be sweating a LOT) and, although considered to be harmless at such minute levels, the fact is that with each washing a little bit of the toxic chemical is retained by the wash water. Testing one of these shirts in the 100 Mile Wilderness showed that the bug repellent material ends up being equally as effective as a similar, lighter, safer shirt with absolutely no treatment whatsoever. Does this mean that I'm right and the marketing is wrong?

One of the most prevalent examples is weight ratings for backpacks. Bottom line is if the label says it can hold 40 pounds; don't believe it until you've researched it. Sometimes just looking at the quality of the seams can tell you whether to believe this value or not. Maybe my pack is rated at 40 pounds, and I'm only carrying 35 pounds, but a lot more than 35 pounds of force is generated on those straps if I slip or jump or even jog/run.

And that's my next point - research and reviews are oftentimes inconclusive and opinionated, so you need to do your own testing. If you asked a perfect stranger "How hot is that pepper?" would you trust the answer "It's pretty mild"? Maybe you would, but then you're also taking a risk.

Gear failure?

I owned three backpacks from a very reputable company that I will simply call Company X. You will find their packs in virtually every outfitter in the US. Their name is synonymous with backpacks. All three fell apart in major ways, all related to manufacturing issues.

The suspension (hip and shoulder straps) on the first pack tore apart drastically, and quickly, in the 100 Mile Wilderness. I was only carrying

35 pounds of weight at the time - it was rated at 35 pounds. Fortunately, I was able to use my indispensable dental floss and sewing needle to do a field repair. Manufacturers often gauge the rated weight using mild hiking conditions, and tend to be a little "hopeful," shall we say. Even though I was carrying the maximum the pack was rated for, I would have expected the straps to last more than 3 days.

The replacement I received from Company X was rated at 30 pounds and the suspension actually held up great with 20-32 pounds, but the pack storage area itself (not the suspension) kept tearing seams, even though I wasn't overstuffing it. There was, in fact, a known flaw with their side compression straps and I simply had to stop using them.

Being a glutton for punishment, I decided to buy a newer model from Company X only, to discover it had a manufacturing defect that caused the adjustment buckle on the shoulder strap to rip off. I noticed this problem one day before mine ripped completely and managed to fix it with dental floss. Customer Service apologized and said the defect has already been addressed but that they couldn't send me a new one since their first priority was to get them out to retailers.

Gear failure is perhaps inevitable and you never know how it will manifest. People laughed at me for carrying a sewing needle and dental floss, but seeing as it staved off severe gear failure on two occasions I will never leave it at home. I also carried parachute cord with internal strands of polyester, perfect for turning in to thread for repairs. One lady put a 10 inch rip in her pants and borrowed my needle and "thread" to fix it up. Or some duct tape - good for a thousand uses.

If you're carrying a lighter, maybe you should have some matches as a backup and vice versa. My $0.99 drugstore lighter rusted up on me once and only luck brought it back to life.

In case your footwear fails, or blisters become too painful, maybe you want to carry some lightweight sandals to alternate between.

There are plenty of great outfitters along the Trail, even if they don't come easily or frequently. With the help of friendly locals and business owners you can often find rides to the nearest sporting goods or camp store, if you can't find one in town.

Are you really hiking in those?

I'll admit I got a kick out of wearing sandals for the last 1,000 miles of the Trail, simply because of the reaction I'd get from hikers and non-hikers. The AT for me was about trying out new gear, so instead of my trusty all-leather full height boots, I started with super breathable, lightweight trail-runners from Adidas and loved the difference. However, they had miserable traction and even on flat, dry ground I could slide.

So I switched to breathable, lightweight hiking shoes from Merrell with Vibram soles. These were great and I found them more comfortable than even my foam camp clogs. But over time, even with a bigger size, I ran into the problem where the tops of my toes would rub after prolonged periods of rain or puddles. When I hit Maryland, I decided to experiment and buy a pair of Chaco hiking sandals. I'd seen Nobo's with them and had read a lot of positive reviews, so I was anxious to give them a try.

Chaco hiking sandals have built-in arch support, aggressive Vibram soles, and are made for outdoor abuse. Throw on a pair of socks to help prevent chafing from the straps, and cushion against sticks and thorns, and you have the perfect footwear.

During the first few weeks with my Chaco's, the tops of my toes healed, the numbed nerves in my toes slowly regained feeling, my toe nails began to grow again, my big toes no longer felt as if they were asleep and, because my feet were always exposed to the air, I could wear one pair of socks for two weeks at a time before they smelled bad. I didn't even stumble or roll my ankle any more than I had before.

There were, however, downsides. Because there was so much rain in the beginning of my hike, I permanently had messed up calluses. Wearing sandals keeps your feet dry, but can also dry them out too much. As a result, my calluses cracked apart painfully and by the time I realized this was happening, it was too late.

At first, I thought I just had cuts and that they'd heal on their own. Then I realized it was actually from dry skin and I bought an array of foot crèmes that did help a lot - but progress could be halted by cold, dry weather or a wet spell followed by dry winds. I battled with open, cracked calluses for the rest of the trip, then for a week on the salty, sandy beaches of Florida (ouch!), and then for about another month of civilian life before they finally became just a memory.

Believe it or not, another downside is that Chaco's weigh more than my Merrell's - but are still lighter than full-size boots. I suppose it's a sign of a sturdy product, but usually one doesn't think "heavy" when they hear the word "sandals."

The last downside is that, yes, you do have to deal with pebbles, rocks, acorns and sticks getting between your feet and the sandal - but this isn't too terribly annoying and eventually you learn how to remove them quickly with a flick of the foot.

For 1,000 miles I wore my Chaco's, occasionally hiking in my foam knock-off Crocs, and no matter which pair I was hiking in, passers-by would often give me that look that says "Are you really wearing those?" Often I would hear from the women, "Oh, honey, the trail ahead is rough, you really should switch back to your hiking shoes," not realizing that these were my hiking shoes, or that the trail is "rough" in both directions. The men would usually just mumble something about how times change and "in my day..."

Things have indeed changed a lot with footwear, even in my short time on this planet. The traditional belief had been that, the taller and stiffer the boot, the better the ankle support. We now realize that the extra weight of a boot puts a lot of strain on the knee, a trade-off some people don't want. "But I'll roll my ankle!" you say? I've rolled my ankle just many times in

After about 900 miles my Chaco's finally kicked the bucket. I repaired them by punching holes in the soles and resecuring the straps with zip ties. On the right is the new pair that replaced them!

boots as I have wearing sneakers or even in sandals. Some people believe it's not the height of the footwear that affects support but the width of the sole. Boots do tend to have wider soles giving them stability but so do my Chaco's.

While boots are awfully good at protecting your feet from rocks, sticks and other factors that might cause injury, you won't have much of that to worry about on the AT - unless you decide to go bushwhacking through the woods for some reason. True, I was more exposed to these things in my sandals and tended to jab my toes with little branches, but it never broke skin or caused any lasting discomfort. You'll be fine with trail-runners; you might even be fine in sandals.

My Croc's were certainly comfortable for short stretches, the lack of a firm sole meant that the pounding of each step was felt all the more and after a few miles the bones of my feet would begin to feel bruised.

Another thing to look at is just how much your body is going to change as you put on the miles. Your ankles are going to strengthen, your agility is going to improve, and any need you might have had for tall ankle support will disappear. My boots are now relegated to the back of the closet where they wait for winter.

But honestly, footwear is not the same for everyone. With a 30 pound pack on my 155 pound body while I was wearing my Merrell's, I could feel the rocks so much more than with the Chaco's. Does that mean everyone should wear Chaco's? No, it's possible that if I were lighter, the Merrell's would actually be a better option. In contrast, if I were carrying more weight, I might actually be better off with my heavy leather boots.

Be prepared to change footwear on the Trail, in case what you're wearing doesn't work out and I'd urge you to at least try hiking in some lightweight low-tops.

Where are your poles?

If I had a dime for every time I was asked why I wasn't hiking with poles, I'd have lots of dimes to throw at people asking me this question! Then I'd pick the coins up to reload!

Poles are an interesting concept and like a lot of things they seem to be marketing hype. Someone once said (and I'm glad to repeat it here) that he felt most people claimed to absolutely love their poles simply because to say otherwise would make them feel foolish for having spent $100 on something so useless.

Before I go any further, let me say that I started off with poles - cheap, old, abused ski poles. I used them for the 100 Mile Wilderness, and then bought a pair of collapsible trekking poles and continued to the Mahoosuc Notch (175 miles) and thought I loved them. Heck, everybody had them, and I paid $100 for them, so it seemed logical then that they HAD to work.

When I reached the Mahoosuc Notch I lashed them to my pack since they'd only get in my way as I scrambled over and under large boulders. Passing immediately into New Hampshire, I kept up the momentum and decided to do the notoriously harsh terrain of New Hampshire without them as well.

For about half of Vermont I switched back to them as a final test, before ultimately liberating myself from them for the final 1,600 miles.

The opinion I developed was that, much like ankle support, as long as I built up the muscles, my legs will support me just fine. I also believe that my stride was more natural without poles and thus had less strain on the knee. This was particularly evident on steep downhills where, without poles, I would crouch or slide on my backside rather than take awkward steps and lean on my poles.

But many factors play into the use of poles and I will gladly point out that I'm in shape, I'm not carrying a heavy pack, I'm not overweight, I have naturally strong knees (and recent physical therapy for ACL replacement surgery made my knees stronger), and I'm young. However, when someone asks if they should get poles, I size them up and base my answer on their age and fitness level. I do believe that most young people claim they love their poles simply because it seems like they should.

At a picnic table in the south, a Leki pole distributor (a popular pole manufacturer) told me that, while my knees felt fine, I was doing long term damage and I should be using poles. This reminds me of the water drinking craze that seemed to come from nowhere in the 90's. How everyone seemed to be carrying water everywhere they went, as if nobody was ever hydrated before. Now, somehow, life depends on bottled water and spring water. Some people claim that, as a preventative measure, poles stave off wear-and-tear, while others claim strengthening the knee is prevention enough. As far as I can tell, nobody knows for sure, and until they do I'll stand on the cheaper and less market-driven side.

"You're wrong; my poles have saved my life too many times to count!" This comment amuses me to no end. What I found with my pole experiment was that, when I had them, I was more likely to take chances, walk faster on a single plank suspended over a bog, or take longer strides going downhill. And, gee, somehow I found myself falling or slipping frequently and relying on my poles to save me. Without them, however, I walked more naturally, had greater balance, slipped less often, and only once in 1,600 miles without poles did I actually fall.

I did find them awfully useful for jumping over large mud puddles or small streams. Ironically, in those same muddy stretches, I also found them to get in the way of my mosquito-swatting efforts.

I say all of this in the hopes that you will try hiking with and without them just to see what YOU think before you drop the cash on a pair. I also found that my $15 aluminum ski poles worked just as well as my $100 collapsibles and wished that I hadn't bought into the hype of "fancy equals better."

25. A Walk in Tennessee & North Carolina

A view from a fire lookout tower just up the hill from the Nantahala Outdoor Center.

Length:	288 miles	464 km
Max Elevation:	6,625 feet	2,019 m
Min Elevation:	1,326 feet	404 m
My First Day:	October 8	
My Last Day:	October 26	

What's it like?

It's nearly impossible to talk separately about North Carolina and Tennessee as the Trail not only crisscrosses the border of the two states but, on a map, the Trail literally follows the border step for step. Elsewhere on the AT, you are greeted with signs welcoming you to a state but not in Tennessee and North Carolina. Because the trail changes states so often, it would be futile to put a sign up every time you left/entered the state, so you are left guessing.

There is one subtle clue to your whereabouts, if ever you find yourself wondering. The caretakers of the Tennessee portion of the AT will not allow privies to be dug as they believe that the waste will not break down sufficiently due to the high elevation. You are forced to dig your own cat hole. So, if you look around at a shelter and you see an outhouse, that means you are in North Carolina. There is, however, a rumor that this policy is changing.

The Tennessee and North Carolina section is truly spectacular, and it probably has something to do with the fact that you are always in a national forest - Cherokee National Forest, Smoky Mountains National Park and Nantahala National Forest. Even when you are in a town, you are still surrounded by federal lands.

The elevations are high here, which can make for awfully cold weather. But it also makes for some stunning views, with or without fall foliage, and it's part of the reason why the south has their famous bald mountains. The Trail feels primitive and historic and the towns are situated in rustic valleys or gaps. The thick oak trees stand tall and grandiose, dropping their acorns to form blankets that cover the ground. Here you can even find mountains referred to as "domes."

In fact, the only problems you're likely to encounter in the Tennessee and North Carolina corridor are related to the trees. The acorns will fall in such quantities that they will collect in depressions on the trail to such depths that you will find yourself rolling, slipping and sliding instead of walking. They are nature's ball bearings and I can't even imagine how many times my feet tried to escape from underneath me.

The other problem here is that the ground is so hard and rocky on the ridgetop sections of the AT that the trail depression isn't all that deep. Falling leaves have no problem filling in all the gaps and forming a uniform, flat looking surface. Northbounders don't have any trouble finding their way because the leaves haven't fallen yet and there are plenty of people to help keep the depression visible. As such, the white blazes tend to be spaced quite far apart since they're not as important for navigation. By the time I arrive in early October, with so few hikers sharing the Trail it becomes quite difficult to identify it in the absence of a blaze. Fortunately, nature has clearly defined the ridges so it would be easy to turn around and walk until I found a blaze if I ever felt myself off course. My biggest fear was that I would lose time retracing my steps, if the Trail decided to turn and head off the ridge without me.

Fall foliage began, for me, in Virginia but it wasn't until Tennessee and North Carolina that it hit its peak. Unlike New England, with its bold, red maple leaves, this part of the country primarily (explicitly?) sees only yellows and oranges. When I arrived in Smoky Mountains National Park, the leaves were at their best and there was a carpet of color, unrolled across the landscape as far as the eye could see. Of course, this also meant troves of people carpeting the trails and park facilities.

The drought was at its worst here and I heavily relied on the locals putting out water at road crossings. Being one of the first Sobo's to hit this region, I told everyone I could about the water problem, just as the hikers in front of me did. Later, I compared my experience with sev-

Fall foliage in the Smokies. What, you can't see the colors in a black and white photo?

eral hikers behind me and learned that, whether from our intervention or happenstance, they found an abundance of bottled water at nearly every Trail access point. Thank you locals!

Just like in Virginia, I encountered many hunters here looking for squirrel and deer. I also met several groups of men walking around with hound dogs that were practicing, or warming up, for bear season. As it happens, one hiker I met said a hound dog visited him at a shelter, with no sign of his owners nearby. Being a highly valued canine, this hunting hound was equipped with a tracking collar and the next morning the owners showed up at the shelter to claim him.

New England is certainly full of coyotes but I don't remember hearing any while hiking there. I did, however, hear a large pack, seemingly just down the hill from a shelter in Tennessee and North Carolina. They were going on and on with that coyote howl of theirs.

A few highlights

Any of the grassy balds on the AT are alluring to say the least. A few that come to mind are Max Patch, Hump Mountain and the balds surrounding Roan Mountain (Round Bald, Jane Bald, Grassy Ridge). They offer panoramic views, warming exposure to the sun, and a chance to see a unique ecosystem. Why are balds so special? When you stand on a bald, you can look around and see other mountains that are taller and yet are fully forested. Mountains in New England have no trees on top either, but that's to be expected due to their cold winters, short summers, high winds and rocky nature. But in the south the conditions are right for forests to grow and yet these balds can't seem to sustain anything bigger than grasses and scrub. You can take photos of Roan High Knob from the top of the adjacent Round Bald, but when you stand on the top of Roan High Knob you can't see anything through the dense forest of fir trees.

Hump Mountain is already on the highlight reel for being a bald, but it also receives special attention because of the long-horned cattle that graze on its summit, alongside horses.

You can't say enough good things about the great Smoky Mountain National Park. The views are outstanding, especially during the peak of fall foliage, as I found out, and while there are a lot of people in the park they tend to cluster around the sites that are close to a parking lot. The more accessible shelters may fill up, but since I was still hanging my hammock in the woods, it wasn't a problem. Bears are known to frequent the shelters during the Northbounder season and are quite the nuisance due to years of campers intentionally and unintentionally feeding them.

At the shelters along the AT, the rule is that you can camp anywhere as long as you are within site of the lean-to. When taken literally, this means you can stay on a ridge two miles away, as long as you can still see the roof of the shelter. I'm pretty sure that's not what the park intended.

If you're looking for something specific to see, then it would have to be Clingman's Dome, the highest point on the Appalachian Trail and the second highest point in the Appalachian Mountains at 6,643 feet (2,025 m). If you choose to, you can park in a large parking lot and walk up a brief, but steep, half-mile paved pathway to the cement lookout tower at the top.

Walking across one of the Tennessee and North Carolina balds.

While not necessarily for the purpose of hiking, I do highly recommend visiting Fontana Dam just outside of Fontana Village. The Trail comes down out of the Smokies and drops you on to a road that leads to the dam by way of a very scenic shoreline. I was passing through in the middle of a drought, considered the worst since they began recording in 1889 and the lake was far below the actual shoreline. This was the year that Atlanta, Georgia, was worried they would run out of water.

Despite the water shortage, the river running through the Nantahala Outdoor Center (or NOC, or En-Oh-See) seemed to have a good flow and it looked like they were still running rafting and kayak trips. I loved stopping here; it's just such a perfectly situated spot on the river. The food at the concession stand is top notch and the outfitter very accommodating. This is where I was able to exchange my broken Chaco's (the straps finally gave out after 900 miles of use) for a new pair since I was still in the warranty phase of ownership. Rather than ship them back to the manufacturer for repair, the outfitter was able to work out a deal where they simply gave me any pair off the shelf and then returned mine for me. I also paid a surprise visit to someone that had been interested in buying ad space on a white-water canoe website I run but hadn't been motivated enough to make it happen. There has to be an easier way to close deals like that than hiking 2,000 miles, but it certainly made it memorable for the both of us.

The Nantahala Outdoor Center where you can get supplies, food, and new Chaco's!

26. Life After

Any advice? What would you do differently?

The irony is that, while you're hiking and camping for more than four months, you rarely see the stars. More often than not, you find yourself going to bed as soon as the sun sets because it's just logical - no need to use precious flashlight battery life or use energy to build a fire. The exception would be staying up late, talking with your fellow hikers. In the middle of the night, if you're lucky enough to be camped in an area where the trees aren't blocking out the sky, you might get up to urinate and have a beautiful view overhead.

While my hammock might have had a screened-in top, capable of letting me see what's above me, the fact is it had to be strung up between two trees, which meant all I saw was a canopy of leaves while lying in bed. I was definitely jealous of tent campers who could set up in a field or on a bald mountain and look up through their mesh roof. For parts of the south, a tent definitely would have been nice.

Try to be realistic, not optimistic, when planning your budget. The hikers I knew with financial troubles simply didn't plan on how much they'd be spending in town - whether you want to hang out with friends or you simply need more food/drink for health AND morale purposes. It's very hard to avoid those temptations and, only a few weeks in, I knew people that were already over-budget and near broke because their plan was to never stay in town, never eat in a restaurant, and live off of cheap trail foods. Many people in this situation will stop hiking, find a temporary job to restore their bank account, then take to the Trail again.

Bring a notepad and use it! I used my Wingfoot Trail Guide to highlight every place I stopped for the night, while my journal was where I'd write about the experiences or highlights of the day. I would often receive information about the location of a restaurant or new, unpublicized hostel, several hundred miles in advance and just figure I'd hear about it again or I'd remember. I rarely remembered and wished I had written it down somewhere (which was annoying because I had a notepad!!!). I can't even count the number of times I would think to myself something like: "What was it I heard about Rusty's Hard Time Hollow - that I should avoid it or that I have to check it out?"

I know people that completed their thru-hike and returned just days later to school or work. Now, I'm not saying it can't be done, but I really wouldn't recommend this approach. After months without a real schedule, deadlines, rules, homework, or a rigid routine, I definitely needed some time off after the AT - as strange as that may sound. I had to let my body adjust to civilization and the lack of complete freedom. I just wanted to eat and relax for a few weeks (at least).

How did you readjust to society?

At first it wasn't easy to readjust to society and as time went by it evolved into something entirely different but equally as difficult.

Even more so than before (even for someone living in a big city), I no longer had the patience to wait for a crosswalk signal. I wasn't used to having to wait for permission to walk, so I'd quite anxiously look for even the smallest of breaks in traffic and would leave my wife behind to wonder why her husband thought it sensible to run through traffic.

Walking down a busy sidewalk, inside a busy store or on the subway platform, I would impatiently dodge through the masses of people - again leaving my wife behind, probably wondering how far I'd get before realizing she was no longer with me. She wasn't a big fan of this side of me.

That behavior eventually faded. A lot of thru-hikers have to worry about returning to civilization and packing on the pounds, due to the desire to continuously eat. Fortunately, I found a job where biking to the office was the quickest way to get there and I was able to run one or two days a week to mix it up. I was therefore able to slowly wean myself off the high calorie diet, rather than be forced to quit cold-turkey or give in to the weight gain.

The hardest part about being off the Trail is when I see something that reminds me of my hike. It generates an almost unbearable burst of nostalgia. It really doesn't take much to trigger these emotions. If I'm driving or biking along some random road and I see some high-tension power lines going up a mountain, it reminds me of all the times the AT followed or crossed a stretch of similar lines and I can smell the tall, dry, sun-drenched grasses and fragrant earth typical of the area around the power lines.

While riding my bicycle on a paved trail one day, I came across a painted box turtle, like the two I hiked past in Virginia, and I just wanted to drop my bike and start walking in to the woods.

Often I will see a cleared field with some dead trees and my heart strings get a little tug; looking at a stream as I'm driving over it; seeing a Snickers bar in a convenience store; walking past someone in a city or town carrying a backpack; a pair of Croc shoes.

And when the feeling hits, I want nothing more than to throw on the backpack and hit the hills. It goes beyond simple desire - it truly comes from the depths of the soul.

What's next?

At the time I finished the AT, my plan was to head back to civilization, normalcy and find a job. I didn't really have any big plans for the future. I'm not sure what the next big adventure will be, but I do have a few likely options.

One option is to hop on a bicycle and pedal around the US for a few months. It's hard to say what route I'd take since the beauty of a bicycle is that you can pretty much go anywhere and still find food/water within a reasonable distance. I may go coast-to-coast or possibly a big, sideways "S", from Maine to the Canadian Rockies then south along the Rockies to New Mexico, over to California and up to Seattle - or in reverse.

And there are other trails I'd like to try, like the Pacific Crest Trail that goes from the Mexican border in California up to the Canadian border in Washington, taking you through desert to the snow-capped Sierra Nevada. At 2,650 miles in length, it is certainly longer than the AT but I anticipate it would take me about the same amount of time, due to the easier grade of the trail and by carrying lighter gear. It would require more planning, since mail drops are necessary for certain stretches, and there are pretty much no shelters and fewer trail towns. Compared to the AT, fewer people attempt to hike it, even fewer go southbound, and it's much more remote. On the other hand, it's also much more beautiful and scenic and dramatic.

I wouldn't mind tackling some of the smaller trails out there, like the little-known Tuscarora - Big Blue Trail. It is 250 miles in length and goes from the AT in Pennsylvania to Maryland, West Virginia and connects up to the AT in Shenandoah National Park, Virginia. It was originally designed as a new route for the AT but was railroaded by other options and eventually fell into disuse and forgotten. Recently it was re-opened and is starting to get some attention.

The Long Trail in Vermont is well-known by AT thru-hikers as it shares the same ground for the southern portion of the state. At 270 miles in length, it follows the Green Mountains from Massachusetts to Canada and is a popular New England hike.

There are too many options to enumerate but these at least are the most likely candidates.

27. A Walk in Georgia

A hazy morning view from the Georgia "green tunnel."

Length:	76 miles	122 km
Max Elevation:	4,461 feet	1,360 m
Min Elevation:	2,510 feet	765 m
My First Day:	October 26	
My Last Day:	October 30	

What's it like?

Georgia is a good first state for Northbounders because the elevation changes aren't drastic, the trail is wide (probably because it has to be), there's a great outfitter with shuttle service just 31 miles in, and it's not far from the food and services at the Nantahala Outdoor Center. For Northbounders it's also a great introduction to just how monotonous the Trail can be – and why Georgia gets lumped together with Massachusetts for being one of the two "green tunnels."

Looking back through my photos, it looks like there were only five places where I had a good view of the surrounding hills. The most memorable being from the first white blaze on Springer Mountain – but not so much for the view as it was the fact that I was done!

It is, in fact, very anti-climatic to end on Springer Mountain. Northbounders reaching the final white blaze on Mount Katahdin are treated to the most spectacular view on the AT, having completed one of the most memorable climbs to get there – one that includes streams, foot bridges, rock scrambling, two exposed alpine summits, and possible moose sightings. In contrast, Springer Mountain is just one small mountain in amongst a range of similar mountains, with no real view except where a few trees seem to have gone missing. There's nothing particularly notable about the georgraphy to make you realize you've reached the end. Thankfully, at least there are some really nice plaques secured to some large rocks that make for some nice photos and a good way to remember the end of the Trail. And then, just like Katahdin, you still have to hike several miles to get to a road or car or however you're getting home.

I can't help but compare Katahdin to Springer. Both are located in state parks (Baxter and Amicalola, respectively) but for Katahdin your only options are camping or catching a ride immediately. Amicalola is kind enough to support a large hotel with great views and three buffet meals a day! On my last day I hiked 31 miles to Springer Mountain and then decided to hike 6 miles (5 miles in the dark) to the hotel, in the hopes that they had a room. That was my longest mileage day and I was so pumped up with adrenaline that I wasn't even tired when I got to the hotel.

On the side trail that you take from the park visitor center to the start of the AT there are signs indicating distance and time to Springer Mountain.

On a side trail in Amicalola State Park is this sign informing northbound hikers how far they are from the start of the AT on Springer Mountain.

Since I was properly conditioned by the Trail at this point, rather than the six hours suggested by the sign, it took me about two hours. I'm sure a Northbounder in good shape, and carrying a light pack, could easily hike the section in three hours.

A few highlights

Amicalola State Park is a really gorgeous place – but then, I'm a sucker for waterfalls. The primary parking lot is next to a well-run visitor center (this is where the official hiker sign-in and sign-out ledger is) at the base of several very tall waterfalls, each accessible by either trails or a well manicured series of wooden steps and boardwalks. The park has a large number of side trails in addition to the AT and the woods here are as good as they get.

If you're like me, you'll love the Mountain Crossings at Walasi-Yi outfitter in Neels Gap 31 miles north of Springer Mountain. Apart from being a great place to stop and stock up, it's on a part of the mountain range that has a good view. As you climb up out of the gap the view stays with you until you reach the top and re-enter the woods. It's a nice short hike.

Mountain Crossings at Walasi-Yi in Neels Gap. A superb outfitter and limited supply point.

28. In Closing

Having hiked 2,200 miles, over the course of 137 days, across 14 states, and two seasons, I am glad to be done, grateful for all the support I received along the way, thankful for all the positive memories and experiences, and enjoying the thought of my next great adventure.

I met many wonderful people along the way, witnessed sights both rare and common, treaded carefully over many ecosystems, examined the change of landscape over time and the varying cultures that come with it.

One of the two plaques on top of Springer Mountain marking the official start/end of the AT in Georgia.

Perhaps most importantly, I gained confidence in myself and my ability to endure the physical and mental trials that are part of long-distance hiking. Oh, right, also that I can subsist for weeks at a time on nothing more than whatever I can find at a gas station convenience store. I am ready for the zombie apocalypse!

For many Southbounders, the plaques embedded in the rock at the top of Springer Mountain, next to the last white blaze, are the final images they'll have of the Appalachian Trail. For many it will be the visitor center in Amicalola State Park, where they officially sign themselves out, after signing in many months ago in Baxter State Park. Or perhaps it's the conflicting sadness and joy they felt when they made that transition from the last AT white blaze to the first blue blaze of the access trail.

For me it's a combination of all these, but none of them can sum up what the AT means.

For that, I need to recall the signs on the AT access trail that inform fresh northbound hikers just how far they have to go on their first day. It's a reminder that not everyone hikes at the same pace, and that some people may finish physically stronger than when they started. It tells us that, no matter who you are, you need to carry the right baggage (literally and figuratively). It also serves as a reminder of the daunting task these individuals are undertaking. Mentally, you suddenly hit a wall and start to do the math. "Gosh, if it takes me six hours to walk seven miles, that means I won't hit civilization at Neels Gap for 40 hours! That's four days of hiking! And that means seven months to Maine!!!" This is probably enough to cause some people - hiking in bad weather, out of shape, with too much gear - to turn around before even hitting the first white blaze. Above all, it's a sanity check as you ask yourself "Am I capable of enduring this day after day?"

The second plaque on top of Springer, letting me know I was done!

For me, the AT was all about time, patience and perspective. I will forever remember it through my photos, stories and friendships.

A sequence of photos I took, just minutes after leaving the summit of Springer Mountain.

From top to bottom, I'm saying: "Yup, I'm done," "I made it alright," "the AT was a piece of cake."

Appendix: Other Books

Here are some of the books I read before hiking the Appalachian Trail, along with my own personal review.

Luxenberg, Larry. *Walking the Appalachian Trail.* Stackpole Books, 1995.

A good overview of the Trail, telling the story through examples, helping to keep a tight perspective. It is very informative and factual while remaining interesting at the same time.

Mueser, Roland. *Long Distance Hiking: Lessons from the Appalachian Trail.* Ragged Mountain Press, 1998.

Great background for those about to hike the AT. It's written like a PhD thesis with tables, statistics, and expert analysis using data from the 1990's, which was a very different era on the AT.

Bryson, Bill. *A Walk in the Woods.* Crown Publishing Group, 1999.

This is the book that introduced many people to the AT. It details the history of the Trail and the experiences of a thru-hiker in an entertaining way.

Curran, Jan D. *The Appalachian Trail: How to Prepare For & Hike It.* Rainbow Books, 2002.

Informative and detail oriented. Good to read before setting off on the Trail, but not something a non-hiker would particularly benefit from.

Chase, Jim. *Guide to the Appalachian Trail.* Stackpole Books, 2005.

I bought this because it goes into details not found in any of the other books - specifically geology and American history.

Appendix: Website

Modern technology allowed me to maintain a website for people to track my progress. I made use of Google Maps to plot my progress. This website was updated approximately 40 times with either points on the map, new photos, or blog entries describing what I've been experiencing.

Kenneth's Appalachian Trail Adventure 2007

| AT 2007 Overview | Status (Map) | Status (Blog) | Gear List | Contact Me |

Introduction
In mid-June 2007 I will begin hiking the Appalachian Trail from Maine to Georgia. This web page contains information and details relevant to this adventure, and I'd recommend you start by reading the pamphlet I've put together (right there, beneath this sentence).

Overview Pamphlet
This pamphlet was written as an overview for friends and family, it answers many common questions.
- PDF Format

How to Reach Me On The Trail
Generally speaking I will not rely on mail drops for supplies, so I will not make a regular habit of checking for mail when I reach a town. Below are some guidelines I'd ask that you follow if you choose to write or send care packages along the way - thanks for caring!

- **Check my status (map or blog) for any requests I might have and especially for mail drop locations!**
- This page will give you a good perspective
- Letters and postcards always welcome!
- Send only small portions
- If sending food, store in freezer style ziplocs, feel free to include a few extra bags too. This goes for homemade as well as store-bought (even things like candy bars or Pez!)
- Have fun and try to surprise me! Just please be sensible, I'll either have to carry it or eat it. :)

The Aftermath
No matter how far I get, I'm sure I'll have lots to write about and plenty of images to provide. Rest assured I will be writing about and making available my story! Keep checking back!

Books and Reviews
I found all of these books to be at least sufficiently well written and generally well edited. The reviews I provide are more focused on relevance and personal likes.

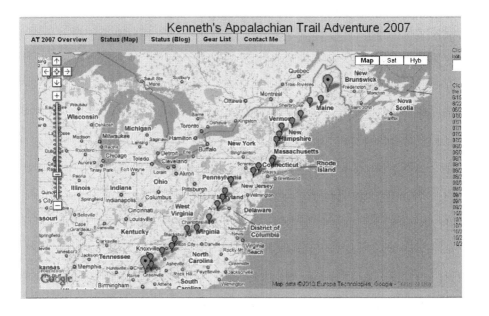

About the author

Building upon a youth spent camping with the Boy Scouts, Ken Sarzynski is an outdoors enthusiast with a penchant for solo bicycle touring, solo backpacking, team mountain biking, and participating in various endurance races. Ken is the co-founder and maintainer of CBoats.net, the world's largest online community for whitewater canoe enthusiasts.

A born-and-raised upstate New Yorker, Ken graduated with baccalaureate degrees in Computer Science and Performing Arts from Colby College in Waterville, Maine. He now resides in the Washington, DC area with his wife and their super-adorable cat, Mao.

Since hiking the AT, Ken has helped educate individuals on the Appalachian Trail with the help of a self-produced DVD movie about his hike. He enjoys helping friends, co-workers and strangers find places to go hiking or camping. He has a natural "I work here" look and regularly finds himself being solicited for advice by shoppers at local outfitters. Even knowing he wasn't an employee, he helped a Russian fellow purchase a backpack for a hiking trip in India, and a lady in need of a new bicycle helmet.

14973432R00118

Made in the USA
Lexington, KY
01 May 2012